From our Kitchen to Yours

Our Best Quick & Easy Casseroles

No-stress recipes for family meals, holiday celebrations, church suppers & more!

*To everyone who
loves cooking for
family & friends!*

Gooseberry Patch
An imprint of Globe Pequot
246 Goose Lane
Guilford, CT 06437

www.gooseberrypatch.com
1 800 854 6673

· · · · · · · · · · · · · · · · · · · ·

Do you have a tried & true recipe...
tip, craft or memory that you'd like to
see featured in a **Gooseberry Patch**
cookbook? Visit our website at
www.gooseberrypatch.com and
follow the easy steps to submit
your favorite family recipe.

Or send them to us at:
Gooseberry Patch
PO Box 812
Columbus, OH 43216-0812

Don't forget to include the number
of servings your recipe makes, plus
your name, address, phone number
and email address. If we select your
recipe, your name will appear right
along with it...and you'll receive a
FREE copy of the book!

CONTENTS

Easy
Family-Favorite
Casseroles

Our Best Quick & Easy Casseroles

Casseroles are what comfort food is all about. They are budget-friendly, perfect for busy weeknights, potlucks, Sunday family get-togethers... really, anytime of day or night! The best part is that they are easy to make, can be made in advance, and the leftovers are delicious. Oh, and they freeze well too!

Here are a few tips to help make casseroles your go-to recipes in the kitchen:

- Turn any casserole into an overnight time-saver. Simply prepare a favorite recipe the night before, cover and refrigerate. The next day, just add 15 to 20 extra minutes to the baking time.

- Free up your favorite baking pan when putting a made-ahead recipe in the freezer. Line the pan with aluminum foil, add recipe ingredients, wrap and freeze...lift out the frozen casserole and return to the freezer. To serve, slip it back into the same pan and bake.

- Shopping for a new casserole dish? Consider getting a deep 13"x9" glass baking pan. It retains heat well to create crisp golden crusts, cleans up easily and can be used for both savory mains and sweet desserts.

- Glass or dark baking pans will retain more heat than shiny ones. Unless the recipe specifies a glass pan, be sure to reduce the oven temperature by 25 degrees when using them.

- Two for one! Double a favorite side dish and freeze half. Another night, turn the remaining portion into a main dish by adding some meat to it. Salsa rice with cubed chicken, baked beans with sliced sausage and macaroni & cheese with diced ham are just a few tasty ideas.

- Baking more than one pan at a time? Remember to stagger them on the oven racks so the food will cook evenly.

South-of-the-Border Dip, Page 20

CHAPTER ONE

Hot Dips & Appetizers

Spinach-Artichoke Dip, Page 26

Hawaiian Bowl Dip, Page 24

Cindy Snyder, Kittanning, PA

Cheddar Apple Pie Dip

This is a great appetizer for a fall gathering of friends around a toasty fire. I also like to serve it at family gatherings. I serve it with whole-grain crackers or small pieces of toasted whole-grain bread.

Makes 8 servings

1/4 c. brown sugar, packed
1/4 t. cinnamon
1 red apple, cored and finely chopped
1 Granny Smith apple, cored and finely chopped
1/2 c. pecan pieces, coarsely chopped

8-oz. pkg. light cream cheese, softened
1-1/2 c. reduced-fat shredded sharp Cheddar cheese
1/4 c. light sour cream

Combine brown sugar and cinnamon in a bowl; stir in apples and pecans. In a separate bowl, mix cream cheese and Cheddar cheese; add sour cream, stirring well to blend. Spread mixture in a 9" pie plate; top with apple mixture. Bake, uncovered, at 375 degrees for 20 minutes, or until heated through.

★ HOT TIP ★ Microwaved baked apples are delicious and oh-so easy. Set a cored apple in a microwave-safe dish, cover with plastic wrap and microwave on high for 4 to 5 minutes, until tender. Top with a sprinkle of brown sugar, cinnamon and a little pat of butter. Heaven!

Cheddar Apple Pie Dip

Emma Brown, Saskatchewan, Canada

Apricot Brie Dip

Creamy and sweet...sure to be a hit at your next party!

Makes 12 servings

1/2 c. dried apricots, finely chopped
1/4 c. apricot nectar or apple juice
1/3 c. plus 1 T. apricot preserves, divided
2-lb. Brie cheese round, rind removed and cubed
bread slices or crackers, cut-up vegetables

Combine apricots, nectar or juice and 1/3 cup preserves in a slow cooker. Cover and cook on high setting for 30 to 40 minutes, until hot. Stir in cheese. Cover and cook on high setting an additional 30 to 40 minutes, until cheese is melted. Stir in remaining preserves. Turn slow cooker to low setting for serving. Serve with bread or crackers and vegetables for dipping.

★ SAVVY SECRET ★ Kitchen shears are so handy for cutting up sticky dried fruit like apricots and dates. Spritzing your shears with a bit of cooking spray first will also help keep fruit from sticking. So easy!

Apricot Brie Dip

Hollie Moots, Marysville, OH

Cheesy Chile Artichoke Dip

This has become a staple at our get-togethers. It's so easy to prepare... and once you've tried it, you can't stop dipping!

Serves 10 to 12

14-oz. jar artichokes, drained
  and chopped
6-1/2 oz. jar marinated artichokes,
  drained and chopped
4-oz. can diced green chiles
1/4 c. mayonnaise
2 c. shredded Cheddar cheese
tortilla chips, snack crackers

Combine artichokes, chiles, mayonnaise and cheese in a bowl; mix well. Transfer to a greased 8"x8" baking pan. Bake, uncovered, at 350 degrees for 20 to 25 minutes, until bubbly and cheese is melted. Serve with tortilla chips and crackers.

David Wink, Gooseberry Patch

Green Chile Chicken Dip

Easy to make and packed with zesty flavor...sure to become your next favorite dip!

Serves 10 to 12

12-oz. can chicken, drained
2 8-oz. pkgs. cream cheese,
  softened and cubed
2 10-3/4 oz. cans cream of chicken
  soup
2 4-oz. cans diced green chiles
4-oz. can diced jalapeño peppers
tortilla chips

In a lightly greased 13"x9" baking pan, combine all ingredients except tortilla chips. Do not drain chiles or peppers. Stir until well blended. Bake, uncovered, at 350 degrees for 20 to 25 minutes, until hot and bubbly. Serve warm with tortilla chips.

Cheesy Chile Artichoke Dip

Lynnette Jones, East Flat Rock, NC

Mapley Appetizers

With traditional Christmas colors from the green pepper and the red maraschino cherries, this is a wonderful holiday appetizer. The recipe was passed down to me by my husband's aunt.

Serves 8 to 10

15-1/4 oz. can pineapple tidbits,
   drained and juice reserved
1/2 c. maple syrup
1/2 c. vinegar
1/3 c. water

4 t. cornstarch
14-oz. pkg. mini smoked sausages
2/3 c. green pepper, cut into
   1" squares
1/2 c. maraschino cherries, drained

In a bowl, blend reserved pineapple juice, maple syrup, vinegar and water; stir in cornstarch. Pour into a slow cooker. Add pineapple and remaining ingredients; stir gently. Cover and cook on low setting for 4 to 6 hours.

★ DOUBLE DUTY ★ Be sure to save the red juice from jars of maraschino cherries. Stir a little of it into lemonade, ginger ale or milk for a sweet pink drink that kids will love.

Mapley Appetizers

Lisa Sett, Thousand Oaks, CA

Jalapeño Popper Dip

Great for parties and watching football games! You'll want to wear a pair of disposable latex gloves when handling the peppers.

Serves 10 to 12

6 to 8 slices bacon, crisply cooked
   and crumbled
2 8-oz. pkgs. cream cheese, softened
1 c. shredded Cheddar cheese
1/2 c. shredded mozzarella cheese
1 c. mayonnaise
4 to 6 jalapeño peppers, seeded and
   chopped

1/4 c. green onion, diced
1 c. round buttery crackers, crushed
1/2 c. grated Parmesan cheese
1/4 c. butter, melted

In a large bowl, combine all ingredients except crackers, Parmesan cheese and butter. Mix well; transfer to a buttered 2-quart shallow casserole dish. Combine remaining ingredients in a separate bowl; sprinkle over the top. Bake, uncovered, at 350 degrees for about 20 to 30 minutes, until hot and bubbly.

★ SAVVY SWAP ★ For a milder or kid-friendly version of this creamy dip, just use mild banana peppers in place of the jalapeños.

Jalapeño Popper Dip

Diana Karol, Dickerson, KS

Kevin's Football Dip

Sunday afternoon football games wouldn't be the same without this hearty dip. Kevin is our son-in-law and the go-to guy for crowd-pleasers. A slow cooker makes this dip so easy!

Serves 10 to 12

1 lb. ground beef
1/2 c. onion, chopped
8-oz. jar taco sauce
10-oz. can diced tomatoes with
    hot peppers
32-oz. pkg. pasteurized process
    cheese spread, cubed
tortilla chips, cubed French bread

Brown beef with onion in a skillet over medium heat; drain. Transfer beef mixture to a slow cooker; add taco sauce, tomatoes and cheese. Cover and cook on high setting for about 45 minutes, stirring every 10 minutes, until cheese is completely melted. Reduce heat to low setting; serve with chips and bread cubes.

Vickie, Gooseberry Patch

Hot Buffalo Dip

This spicy dip features 3 cheeses and is fit for any party. One of my favorite dips...oh-so easy to make and we all love it!

Makes 16 servings

4 6-oz. boneless, skinless chicken
    breasts, cooked and chopped
2 8-oz. pkgs. 1/3-less-fat cream
    cheese, cubed and softened
1 c. hot wing sauce
1/2 c. shredded reduced-fat Cheddar
    cheese
1/4 c. light blue cheese salad dressing

In a slow cooker, mix together all ingredients. Cover and cook on low setting for 3 to 4 hours.

★ DO IT YOURSELF ★ **Make your own baked tortilla chips! Spritz both sides of corn or flour tortillas with non-stick vegetable spray and cut into wedges. Microwave on high setting for 5 to 6 minutes, turning wedges over every 1-1/2 minutes. Sprinkle warm chips with sea salt and serve.**

Kevin's Football Dip

Darcy Geiger, Columbia City, IN

South-of-the-Border Dip

I make this dip for get-togethers... it's very easy and yummy!

Serves 10 to 12

2 lbs. ground pork sausage, browned and drained
3 14-1/2 oz. cans diced tomatoes with green chiles
1 c. favorite salsa
2 c. canned black beans, drained
2 c. canned corn, drained
32-oz. pkg. sharp Cheddar or queso blanco pasteurized process cheese, cubed
8-oz. pkg. cream cheese, cubed
tortilla chips

Combine sausage, tomatoes with juice and remaining ingredients except tortilla chips in a slow cooker; mix gently. Cover and cook on low setting for about 4 hours, until cheeses are melted. Stir before serving. Serve warm with tortilla chips.

Marlene Darnell, Newport Beach, CA

Slow-Cooked Scrumptious Salsa

Nothing beats the taste of fresh, homemade salsa. This recipe is so simple, I make it all the time with fresh produce from my backyard garden. I give it as gifts and make sure to pass the recipe along with it!

Makes 8 servings

10 roma tomatoes, cored
2 cloves garlic
1 onion, cut into wedges
2 jalapeño peppers, seeded and chopped
1/4 c. fresh cilantro, coarsely chopped
1/2 t. salt

Combine tomatoes, garlic and onion in a slow cooker. Cover and cook on high setting for 2-1/2 to 3 hours, until vegetables are tender. Remove crock and let cool. Combine cooled tomato mixture and remaining ingredients in a food processor or blender. Process to desired consistency. May be refrigerated in a covered container for about one week.

South-of-the-Border Dip

Vickie, Gooseberry Patch

Chipotle-Black Bean Dip

I am always asked to take this smoky, spicy bean dip wherever I go...I've even started bringing the recipe to share.

Makes 12 servings

16-oz. can fat-free refried beans
15-oz. can black beans, drained and rinsed
11-oz. can sweet corn & diced peppers, drained
1 c. chunky salsa
2 chipotle chiles in adobo sauce, chopped and 2 t. adobo sauce reserved
1-1/2 c. shredded reduced-fat Cheddar cheese, divided
4 green onions, chopped
9-oz. pkg. multi-grain tortilla chips

Mix together beans, corn, salsa, chiles, reserved adobo sauce and one cup cheese in a slow cooker. Cover and cook on low setting for 3 to 4 hours, stirring after 2 hours. Sprinkle with remaining cheese and onions. Keep warm on low setting; serve with tortilla chips.

★ HOT TIP ★ Spread some Chipotle-Black Bean Dip or warmed refried beans on an open tortilla for a delicious lunch treat! Top with shredded lettuce, a sprinkle of chopped fresh veggies, a bit of shredded cheese and a drizzle of sour cream. Yum!

Chipotle-Black Bean Dip

Sherry Hill, Sylacauga, AL

Hawaiian Bowl Dip

My grandmother and I made this hot dip when I was in my teen years and I have been making it ever since. My family really enjoys it in the cool fall months, just in time for football. It is delicious and easy to make... everyone enjoys it.

Serves 8 to 10

16-oz. loaf Hawaiian sweet
  bread or French bread bowl
8-oz. pkg. cream cheese,
  softened
12-oz. container sour cream
2 c. shredded sharp Cheddar
  cheese
2 c. shredded Cheddar cheese

1 bunch green onions, chopped
2-oz. pkg. deli honey ham,
  chopped
scoop-type corn chips

Place bread in a baking pan. Cut off the top of bread and reserve. Scoop out the inside to make a bowl; set aside. In a bowl, blend cream cheese and sour cream. Fold in remaining ingredients except corn chips. Spoon mixture into hollowed-out bread; replace bread top. Wrap bread completely in foil. Bake at 350 degrees for one hour. Just before serving, remove bread top and stir dip very well. Serve with corn chips.

★ VARIETY FOR FUN ★ **Try serving soups and dips in bread bowls! Scoop out small rye or sourdough bread rounds and brush the insides with olive oil. Bake in a 350-degree oven for 10 minutes, then fill with hearty soup.**

Hawaiian Bowl Dip

Arlene Smulski, Lyons, IL

Spinach-Artichoke Dip

Serve with pita chips and sliced vegetables for dipping.

Makes 16 servings

14-oz. can artichoke hearts, drained and chopped
2 bunches fresh spinach, chopped
2 8-oz. pkgs. 1/3-less-fat cream cheese, softened and cubed
2-1/2 c. shredded Monterey Jack cheese
2-1/2 c. shredded part-skim mozzarella cheese
3 cloves garlic, minced
1/4 t. pepper

Combine chopped artichokes, spinach and cheeses in a slow cooker; mix well. Stir in garlic and pepper. Cover and cook on high setting for about one to 2 hours, stirring occasionally, until cheeses are melted and dip is smooth. Reduce heat to low setting to keep warm.

Jen Burnham, Delaware, OH

Reuben Dip

Add a basket of party rye slices or pumpernickel rye pretzels...
I guarantee it'll be a hit at your next tailgating party!

Makes 6 to 7 cups

16-oz. jar sauerkraut, drained
1/2 lb. deli-style corned beef, shredded
8-oz. pkg. cream cheese, softened
8-oz. pkg. shredded Swiss cheese
1/4 c. Thousand Island salad dressing

Combine all ingredients in a slow cooker. Cover and cook on high setting for 45 minutes, stirring occasionally, just until heated through and cheese is melted.

★ APPETIZE IT ★ **Love Reubens?**
Try these mini Reubens for appetizers or snacks! Cut cheese and corned beef into squares and serve on party rye slices. Instead of grilling, broil open-faced until the cheese is melted.

HOT DIPS & APPETIZERS

Spinach-Artichoke Dip

Suzanne Varnes, Palatka, FL

Confetti Cheesecake

A recipe I have made many times...my guests always enjoy it! Serve it with crisp crackers, or slice thinly and serve with a green salad for a light lunch.

Serves 10 to 12

1-1/2 c. round buttery cracker crumbs
1/2 c. butter, melted
2 8-oz. pkgs. cream cheese, softened
2 eggs
1/3 c. all-purpose flour
8-oz. container sour cream
1-1/2 c. green pepper, finely chopped
3/4 c. carrot, peeled and shredded
1/4 c. onion, finely chopped

1/4 t. salt
1/4 t. white pepper
assorted crackers

Combine cracker crumbs and butter; press into an ungreased 9" or 10" springform pan. Bake at 300 degrees for 10 minutes; remove from oven. In a large bowl, beat cream cheese until fluffy; add eggs, one at a time. Stir in flour, mixing well. Add remaining ingredients except crackers, folding vegetables well into batter. Pour into baked crust; bake at 300 degrees for one hour. Turn oven off; cool in oven for one hour before refrigerating. At serving time, remove outer ring of springform pan. Serve with crackers.

★ TIME-SAVING SHORTCUT ★ Need to soften cream cheese in a hurry? Simply place an unwrapped 8-ounce block on a plate and microwave for about a minute at 50% power.

Confetti Cheesecake

Kathy Grashoff, Fort Wayne, IN

Bacon-Horseradish Dip

Put a slow cooker to work cooking up this creamy, cheesy dip...it's out of this world!

Makes 7 to 8 cups

3 8-oz. pkgs. cream cheese, softened
12-oz. pkg. shredded Cheddar cheese
1 c. half-and-half
1/3 c. green onion, chopped
3 cloves garlic, minced
3 T. prepared horseradish
1 T. Worcestershire sauce
1/2 t. pepper
12 slices bacon, crisply cooked and crumbled
bagel chips or assorted crackers

Combine all ingredients except bacon and chips or crackers in a slow cooker. Cover and cook on low setting for 4 to 5 hours, or on high setting for 2 to 2-1/2 hours, stirring once halfway through. Just before serving, stir in bacon. Serve with bagel chips or crackers.

Pam Lewis, Munster, IN

Baja Bites

Nice 'n spicy tidbits that are oh-so easy to whip up!

Makes 9 servings

5 eggs, beaten
1 c. cottage cheese
1/4 c. all-purpose flour
1/2 t. baking powder
1/4 c. butter, melted
2 T. green onion, minced
4-oz. can diced green chiles, drained
8-oz. pkg. shredded Monterey Jack cheese

Combine eggs and cottage cheese; mix until almost smooth. Add flour, baking powder and butter; stir in onion, chiles and cheese. Pour into a lightly greased 8"x8" baking pan. Bake at 350 degrees for 30 to 40 minutes. Cool slightly; cut into squares.

Bacon-Horseradish Dip

Kiersten Armstead, Cincinnati, OH

Cincinnati-Style Chili Dip

In Cincinnati, it's just not a tailgate party unless this warm dip is being passed around. Try to find a chili with cinnamon for an authentic Queen City experience!

Makes 10 servings

2 8-oz. pkgs. cream cheese, softened
2 10-1/2 oz. cans Cincinnati-style or plain chili without beans
16-oz. pkg. shredded mild Cheddar cheese
tortilla chips

Spread cream cheese in an ungreased 13"x9" glass baking pan. Pour chili over top and sprinkle with cheese. Bake, uncovered, at 350 degrees for 15 to 20 minutes, until cheese is melted. Serve with tortilla chips.

Trudy Williams, Middlesex, NC

Nacho Chicken Dip

We love this delicious dip at parties... it's even good as a meal, paired with a side salad.

Makes about 6-1/2 cups

16-oz. can refried beans
12-oz. can chicken, drained
16-oz. jar chunky salsa
8-oz. pkg. shredded Mexican blend cheese
tortilla chips

Layer beans, chicken, salsa and cheese in a lightly greased one-quart casserole dish. Bake, uncovered, at 350 degrees for 30 minutes, or until cheese is bubbly. Serve hot with tortilla chips.

★ YOUR WAY ★ Serve chili Cincinnati-style! For 2-way chili, ladle chili over a bowl of spaghetti. For 3-way, top chili and spaghetti with shredded Cheddar cheese. For 4-way, spoon diced onions on top of the cheese...add chili beans to the stack for 5-way.

Cincinnati-Style Chili Dip

Jo Ann, Gooseberry Patch

Caramelized Vidalia Onion Dip

Here's a new take on an old favorite appetizer. Look for sturdy sweet potato chips for scooping up this mega-cheesy family favorite.

Makes 4 cups

2 T. butter
3 Vidalia or other sweet onions, thinly sliced
8-oz. pkg. cream cheese, softened
8-oz. pkg. Swiss cheese, shredded
1 c. grated Parmesan cheese
1 c. mayonnaise
sweet potato chips

Melt butter in a large skillet over medium heat; add sliced onions. Cook, stirring often, 30 to 40 minutes or until onions are caramel colored. Combine onions, cheeses and mayonnaise, stirring well. Spoon dip into a lightly greased 1-1/2 to 2-quart casserole dish. Bake, uncovered, at 375 degrees for 30 minutes or until golden and bubbly. Serve with sweet potato chips.

★ SNACK SECRET ★ Homemade sweet potato chips are so easy to make! Peel sweet potatoes and slice thinly, toss with oil and spread on a baking sheet. Place on the center oven rack and bake at 400 degrees for 22 to 25 minutes, turning once. Sprinkle with sea salt or cinnamon-sugar.

Caramelized Vidalia Onion Dip

Janet Schaeper, Pickerington, OH

Warm Blue Cheese & Bacon Dip

Garnish with a sprinkle of extra chives and crispy bacon...irresistible!

Serves 12

1/2 lb. bacon
4 cloves garlic, minced
2 8-oz. pkgs. cream cheese, softened
1/2 c. half-and-half
2 4-oz. containers crumbled blue cheese
1/4 c. fresh chives, snipped
baguette slices, celery stalks

In a skillet over medium heat, cook bacon until crisp. Drain bacon on paper towels. Add garlic to drippings in skillet; sauté until soft, about one minute. Beat together cream cheese and half-and-half with an electric mixer on high speed. Stir in crumbled bacon, garlic, blue cheese and chives; spoon into an ungreased 8"x8" baking pan. Cover and bake at 350 degrees for about 30 minutes, until lightly golden. Serve with baguette slices and celery stalks.

★ CRISPY TREAT ★ Creamy hot dips are twice as tasty with homemade toasted baguette crisps! Thinly slice a loaf of French bread and arrange slices on a baking sheet. Sprinkle with olive oil and garlic powder, then bake at 400 degrees for 12 to 15 minutes.

Warm Blue Cheese & Bacon Dip

Margaret Collins, Clarendon Hills, IL

Chicken-Salsa Dip

Scoop it out with tortilla chips or corn chips...a perfect appetizer for a small gathering!

Serves 8

8-oz. pkg. cream cheese, softened
8-oz. jar salsa, divided
8-oz. pkg. shredded Mexican-blend
  cheese
2 to 3 boneless, skinless chicken
  breasts, cooked and diced
tortilla chips

Blend cream cheese with half of the salsa; spread in the bottom of an ungreased 9" pie plate. Top with remaining salsa; sprinkle with cheese and chicken. Bake, uncovered, at 350 degrees for 25 minutes, until hot and cheese is melted. Serve warm with tortilla chips.

Eli Martinez, El Paso, TX

Hot & Melty Taco Dip

Get the party started with this panful of sassy, cheesy goodness!

Serves 8

16-oz. can refried beans
1-1/2 oz. pkg. taco seasoning mix
16-oz. container sour cream
8-oz. pkg. cream cheese, softened
16-oz. jar salsa
8-oz. pkg. shredded sharp Cheddar
  cheese
Garnish: shredded lettuce, chopped
  tomatoes, sliced black olives,
  jalapeño peppers, green onions
scoop-type tortilla chips

In a bowl, combine refried beans with taco seasoning. Spread in the bottom of a lightly greased 13"x9" glass baking pan; set aside. In a separate bowl, blend sour cream and cream cheese; spread over bean layer. Spoon salsa over sour cream layer; sprinkle cheese on top. Bake, uncovered, at 350 degrees for about 25 minutes, until beans are warmed through and cheese is melted. Garnish with desired toppings. Serve with tortilla chips.

Chicken-Salsa Dip

Chocolate-Chip Oven Pancake, Page 66

CHAPTER TWO

Breakfast & Brunch Bakes

Cream Cheese Enchiladas, Page 60

Strawberry French Toast, Page 74

Amy Ott, Greenfield, IN

Cinnamon Roll Casserole

Ooey-gooey and irresistible! This recipe is great for holiday mornings... just brew the coffee, serve and enjoy.

Serves 6 to 8

2 12-oz. tubes refrigerated
　cinnamon rolls, separated
4 eggs
1/2 c. whipping cream
3 T. maple syrup
2 t. vanilla extract
1 t. cinnamon
1/4 t. nutmeg

Cover the bottom of a greased slow cooker with cinnamon rolls from one tube, adding one or 2 more rolls from remaining tube if necessary. Set aside icing packets. In a bowl, whisk together eggs, cream, maple syrup, vanilla and spices; drizzle over rolls. Break remaining rolls into bite-size chunks; place on top. Spoon one packet of icing over top; refrigerate remaining icing. Cover and cook on low setting for 3 hours, or until rolls are set. Just before serving, drizzle with remaining icing.

Andy Burton, Dublin, OH

Baked Apple Pancake

Mmm...tender apples, brown sugar and cinnamon!

Serves 6 to 8

4 apples, peeled, cored and sliced
1/2 c. butter, softened and divided
1/2 c. brown sugar, packed
1 t. cinnamon
6 eggs, beaten
1 c. all-purpose flour
1 c. milk
3 T. sugar

Combine apples, 1/4 cup butter, brown sugar and cinnamon in a microwave-safe bowl. Microwave on high setting about 2 to 4 minutes, until tender. Stir; spoon into a lightly greased 13"x9" baking pan and set aside. In a separate bowl, combine remaining ingredients; whisk until smooth and spread over apple mixture. Bake, uncovered, at 425 degrees for 25 minutes. Cut into squares; serve warm.

★ FREEZE IT ★ Tuck odds & ends of leftover cinnamon rolls, fruit muffins and doughnuts into a freezer container... they're scrumptious in your favorite bread pudding recipe.

Cinnamon Roll Casserole

Amy Butcher, Columbus, GA

Fluffy Baked Eggs

Who would have thought to combine pineapple and eggs? After you taste this yummy recipe, you'll see why it is our family favorite!

Makes 12 servings

14 eggs, beaten
3 slices bacon, crisply cooked and
   crumbled
1-1/3 c. low-fat cottage cheese
8-oz. can crushed pineapple in own
   juice, drained
1 t. vanilla extract
Garnish: cooked bacon crumbles,
   chopped fresh parsley

Blend together eggs, bacon, cottage cheese, pineapple and vanilla; spoon into a greased 13"x9" baking pan. Bake, uncovered, at 350 degrees for 40 to 45 minutes or until center is set and a toothpick inserted in center comes out clean. Allow baking pan to stand 5 minutes before slicing. Garnish with cooked bacon crumbles and parsley; cut into squares.

Jill Burton, Gooseberry Patch

Baked Eggs in Tomatoes

So pretty for a brunch...a delicious way to enjoy tomatoes from the farmers' market.

Makes 6 servings

6 tomatoes, tops cut off
1/4 t. pepper
1/2 c. corn, thawed if frozen
1/2 c. red pepper, diced
1/2 c. mushrooms, diced
2 T. cream cheese, softened and
   divided
6 eggs
2 t. fresh chives, minced
1/4 c. grated Parmesan cheese

With a spoon, carefully scoop out each tomato, creating shells. Sprinkle pepper inside tomatoes. Divide corn, red pepper and mushrooms among tomatoes; top each with one teaspoon cream cheese. In a bowl, whisk together eggs and chives. Divide egg mixture among tomatoes; top with Parmesan cheese. Place filled tomatoes in a lightly greased 2-quart casserole dish. Bake, uncovered, at 350 degrees until egg mixture is set, about 45 to 50 minutes. Serve warm.

Fluffy Baked Eggs

Marsha Baker, Pioneer, OH

Coconut Pecan Pie Oatmeal

What a wonderful way to begin your day, waking up to a hot breakfast waiting for you. This recipe is perfect for Christmas morning or any busy morning during the holiday rush.

Serves 5 to 6

1 c. chopped pecans
1/2 c. sweetened flaked coconut
1-1/2 c. long-cooking or steelcut oats, uncooked
4-1/2 c. milk
2/3 c. dark brown sugar, packed
2 T. sugar-free cook & serve vanilla pudding mix
1/4 c. butter
1 t. vanilla or coconut extract
Garnish: milk

Place pecans in a small dry skillet over medium heat. Cook until toasted and golden, stirring frequently and watching carefully. Remove pecans to a bowl. Toast coconut in skillet the same way. Reserve half the pecans and coconut for serving. In a slow cooker, combine remaining pecans, coconut and other ingredients; stir. Cover and cook on low setting for 7 to 8 hours. Serve oatmeal in bowls, topped with reserved pecans and coconut and a splash of milk.

Connie Herek, Bay City, MI

Apple & Berry Breakfast Crisp

Use sliced strawberries instead of blueberries and it's just as tasty... and a dollop of vanilla yogurt on top makes it perfect!

Makes 9 servings

4 apples, peeled, cored and thinly sliced
2 c. blueberries
1/4 c. brown sugar, packed
1/4 c. frozen orange juice concentrate, thawed
2 T. all-purpose flour
1 t. cinnamon
Optional: vanilla yogurt

Combine all ingredients except yogurt in a large bowl; stir until fruit is evenly coated. Spoon into a lightly greased 8"x8" baking pan. Sprinkle Oat Topping evenly over fruit. Bake at 350 degrees for 30 to 35 minutes, until apples are tender. Serve warm with yogurt, if desired.

Oat Topping:

1 c. quick-cooking or long-cooking oats, uncooked
1/2 c. brown sugar, packed
1/3 c. butter, melted
2 T. all-purpose flour

Combine all ingredients; mix well.

Coconut Pecan Pie Oatmeal

Melissa Cassulis, Bridgewater, NY

Haystack Eggs

This is one of my dad's favorite breakfast treats. Mom has been making it for him for almost as long as I can remember!

Makes 4 servings

1-3/4 oz. can shoestring potatoes
4 eggs
1 c. shredded Cheddar cheese
6 slices bacon, crisply cooked and
   crumbled

Spread potatoes evenly over bottom of a greased 9" pie plate. Make 4 indentations in potatoes almost to bottom of pie plate. Carefully break one egg into each indentation. Bake at 350 degrees for 8 to 10 minutes, until eggs are almost set. Sprinkle with cheese and bacon. Return to oven; bake 2 to 4 more minutes, until eggs are set and cheese melts. Cut into 4 wedges; serve immediately.

Rebecca Barna, Blairsville, PA

Summer Swiss Quiche

This is an excellent breakfast or brunch dish to serve when the garden harvest kicks in.

Serves 8 to 10

1/2 lb. bacon
2 zucchini, thinly sliced
1 green pepper, chopped
1 onion, chopped
8 eggs, beaten
1 c. milk
1/4 c. biscuit baking mix
6 slices Swiss cheese

Cook bacon in a skillet over medium heat until crisp; remove from pan and set aside. Sauté zucchini, green pepper and onion in bacon drippings in same skillet over medium heat. Mix eggs, milk and baking mix in a bowl. Pour egg mixture into a lightly greased 13"x9" baking pan. Spoon zucchini mixture over egg mixture. Arrange cheese slices on top; cover with crumbled bacon. Bake, uncovered, at 350 degrees for 30 to 35 minutes, until a toothpick inserted in center comes out clean. Cut into squares.

Haystack Eggs

Audra Vanhorn-Sorey, Columbia, NC

Pumpkin French Toast Bake

This recipe is delightful on a cool fall morning. Just pull it from the fridge and bake...the delicious aroma will bring everyone to the breakfast table!

Makes 10 servings

1 loaf crusty French bread, cubed
7 eggs, beaten
2 c. milk
1/2 c. canned pumpkin
2 t. pumpkin pie spice, divided
1 t. vanilla extract
3-1/2 T. brown sugar, packed
Optional: 1/2 c. chopped pecans
Garnish: maple syrup

Spread bread cubes in a greased 13"x9" baking pan; set aside. In a large bowl, whisk together eggs, milk, pumpkin, 1-1/2 teaspoons spice and vanilla. Pour evenly over bread; press down with spoon until bread is saturated. Cover and refrigerate overnight. In the morning, uncover and top with brown sugar, remaining spice and pecans, if desired. Bake, uncovered, at 350 degrees for 35 to 45 minutes, until golden. Serve with maple syrup.

Jennie Gist, Gooseberry Patch

Blueberry French Toast

A new and yummy twist on French toast for the whole family to enjoy.

Makes 6 servings

2 c. fresh or frozen blueberries
2 T. cornstarch
1/4 c. sugar
1/2 c. orange juice
1/2 c. plus 3 T. water, divided
3 eggs, beaten
6 slices bread
2 T. butter, melted
cinnamon-sugar to taste

Spread blueberries in a greased 13"x9" baking pan; set aside. In a bowl, combine cornstarch, sugar, orange juice and 1/2 cup water; pour over blueberries. In a shallow bowl, whisk together eggs and remaining water. Dip bread slices into egg mixture; arrange over blueberries in pan. Brush bread slices with butter and sprinkle with cinnamon-sugar. Bake, uncovered, at 350 degrees for 15 to 20 minutes, until bread is lightly toasted and sauce is bubbly and thickened. Serve toast slices topped with blueberry mixture from pan.

Pumpkin French Toast Bake

Nick Jenner, Chicago, IL

Sheet Pan Steak & Eggs

I make breakfast for my golf buddies sometimes before we hit the links. Cooking everything in one pan makes clean-up easy.

Serves 3 to 6

2 T. olive oil
2 lbs. potatoes, peeled and diced
4 cloves garlic, minced
1/4 c. grated Parmesan cheese
1/2 t. salt, divided
1/2 t. pepper, divided
2 lbs. beef sirloin steak, sliced into
   1-inch pieces
3 to 6 eggs
Optional: chopped fresh chives

Spread oil on a large rimmed baking sheet; spread potatoes over oil. Sprinkle with garlic and cheese; toss to combine. Sprinkle with half each of salt and pepper. Bake at 400 degrees for 20 to 25 minutes, until potatoes are golden. Remove pan from oven; preheat oven to broil. Season beef with remaining salt and pepper; add to pan in a single layer. With the back of a spoon, create 3 to 6 wells in potato mixture. Gently crack eggs into wells. Broil until egg whites have set and beef is cooked through. Garnish with chives, if desired.

★ TASTY TIP ★ Broiled roma tomatoes make a tasty, quick garnish for steak dishes. Simply place tomato halves cut-side up on a broiler pan. Toss together equal amounts of Italian-seasoned dry bread crumbs and grated Parmesan cheese with a little olive oil. Spoon onto tomatoes and broil until golden.

Sheet Pan Steak & Eggs

Stuart Wilder, Las Vegas, NV

Bacon & Mushroom Baked Omelet

I like to use fresh mushrooms in my omelet, but feel free to sauté them first if you prefer.

Serves 4 to 6

8 eggs, beaten
1/2 lb. mushrooms, sliced
1/2 c. green onion, chopped
4 slices bacon, cooked and crumbled
1 c. shredded Cheddar cheese
salt and pepper to taste

In a large bowl, mix together eggs, mushrooms, onion and bacon. Add salt and pepper to taste. Pour mixture into a greased 8"x8" casserole dish. Sprinkle cheese over top. Bake, uncovered, at 350 degrees for 20 minutes, or until set.

Jessica Dekoekkoek, Richmond, VA

Upside-Down Eggs & Potatoes

Delicious served with grilled breakfast sausages!

Makes 6 servings

2 to 3 T. olive oil
1 to 2 potatoes, shredded
1-1/2 t. garlic powder
1-1/2 t. onion powder
1/2 t. paprika
1-1/2 c. shredded Mexican-blend cheese
6 eggs
salt and pepper to taste
Garnish: sour cream, salsa

Heat oil in a deep 12" oven-proof skillet over medium heat. Pat potatoes dry; add seasonings and toss to mix. Add potatoes to skillet. When about half cooked, use the back of a wooden spoon to smooth out potatoes over the bottom and up the sides of the skillet, to form a crust with no holes. Add cheese in an even layer. Beat eggs very well; add salt and pepper to taste. Gently pour in eggs over cheese. Bake, uncovered, at 375 degrees for 25 to 35 minutes, until a knife tip comes out clean. Carefully unmold onto a serving plate. Let stand for 10 minutes before cutting into wedges. Serve with sour cream and salsa.

Bacon & Mushroom Baked Omelet

Alice Collins, Kansas City, MO

Overnight Apple French Toast

Serve with bacon or sausage on the side, or fresh orange slices and strawberries.

Serves 6 to 8

1 c. brown sugar, packed
1/2 c. butter
2 T. light corn syrup
4 Granny Smith apples, peeled, cored and sliced 1/4-inch thick
3 eggs
1 c. milk
1 t. vanilla extract
9 slices day-old French bread

In a small saucepan, combine brown sugar, butter and corn syrup; cook over low heat until thick. Pour into an ungreased 13"x9" pan, arranging apple slices on top of syrup. In a mixing bowl, beat eggs, milk and vanilla. Dip French bread in egg mixture and arrange over top of apple slices. Cover and refrigerate overnight. Remove from refrigerator 30 minutes before baking and uncover. Bake at 350 degrees for 35 to 40 minutes, until the top of the bread is golden. Serve French toast with apple slices on top, and spoon the warm Sauce on top.

Sauce:

1 c. applesauce
10-oz. jar apple jelly
1/2 t. cinnamon
1/8 t. ground cloves

Combine all ingredients in a saucepan and cook over medium heat until jelly is melted.

★ FLAVOR BURST ★ For extra-special pancakes or French toast, top with homemade maple butter...it's so easy to make! Just blend 1/2 cup butter with 3/4 cup maple syrup.

Overnight Apple French Toast

Liz Plotnick-Snay, Gooseberry Patch

Artichoke-Parmesan Breakfast Casserole

I like to serve this with a green salad when I have friends over for brunch.

Serves 6 to 8

14-oz. can artichokes, drained and
    chopped
3/4 c. shredded Cheddar cheese
3/4 c. shredded Monterey Jack cheese
10 eggs
1 c. sour cream
1/3 c. grated Parmesan cheese
Garnish: salsa

Spread artichokes evenly over bottom of greased 11"x7" casserole dish. Top with Cheddar and Monetery Jack cheeses; set aside. In a large bowl, whisk together eggs and sour cream. Pour over cheese. Top egg mixture with Parmesan cheese. Bake, uncovered, at 350 degrees for 30 to 35 minutes, until set. Garnish with salsa.

Debbie Foster, Eastover, SC

Egg & Mushroom Bake

This hearty dish can be served for breakfast, lunch or dinner!

Makes 4 servings

1 doz. eggs, beaten and scrambled
8-oz. pkg. sliced mushrooms
10-3/4 oz. can cream of mushroom
    soup
2/3 c. milk
8-oz. jar bacon bits
1-1/2 c. shredded Cheddar cheese

Spread eggs in the bottom of a greased 1-1/2 quart casserole dish; top with mushrooms. Set aside. Combine soup and milk in a microwave-safe bowl; heat in a microwave oven on high for 3 minutes, stirring after each minute. Pour over mushrooms; sprinkle with bacon bits and Cheddar cheese. Bake at 350 degrees for 30 minutes.

★ JUST FOR FUN ★ Crunchy toppings can really add fun and flavor to casseroles, chili and soup. Some fun and tasty choices...bacon bits, French fried onions, sunflower seeds and toasted nuts.

Artichoke-Parmesan Breakfast Casserole

Mary Kathryn Carter, Platte City, MO

Cream Cheese Enchiladas

This creamy variation on Mexican enchiladas is yummy! It won me 1st place in a local newspaper's holiday cooking contest. For a brunch twist, use breakfast sausage instead of ground beef.

Makes 8 servings

2 8-oz. pkgs. cream cheese, softened
1 c. sour cream
2 10-oz. cans mild green chile
   enchilada sauce
1/4 c. jalapeños, chopped
1 lb. ground beef, browned and
   drained
1/2 c. shredded sharp Cheddar cheese
8 to 12 flour tortillas
1 sweet onion, chopped
1/2 c. sliced black olives
Garnish: sliced black olives, chopped
   tomato, shredded lettuce, chopped
   green onion

Blend together cream cheese, sour cream, enchilada sauce and jalapeños in a large bowl; set aside. Combine ground beef and shredded cheese in another bowl; set aside. Fill each tortilla with one to 2 tablespoons cream cheese mixture and one to 2 tablespoons beef mixture. Sprinkle each with onion and olives; roll up tortillas. Place in a 13"x9" baking pan; cover with remaining cream cheese mixture. Bake, uncovered, at 400 degrees for 30 to 40 minutes; cover if top begins to brown. Garnish with olives, tomatoes, lettuce and green onions.

★ MAKE IT A PARTY ★ When hosting a brunch for family & friends, make it a potluck with a twist. You provide a hearty main course like enchiladas...others can bring their own specialties like a tossed salad, a veggie dish, yeast rolls and so on. Less work, less expense and more fun for everyone!

Cream Cheese Enchiladas

Nola Coons, Gooseberry Patch

Quick & Easy Cheesy Baked Omelet

This is an easy recipe to customize to your family's tastes. We mix up the flavors quite often!

Makes 4 servings

6 eggs
1/4 c. water
1/2 t. salt
1/4 t. pepper
2 T. butter
1/4 c. green onion, diced
1 c. cooked ham, diced
1 green pepper, diced
1 c. shredded mozzarella cheese
Garnish: sour cream, chopped chives

In a medium bowl, whisk together eggs, water, salt and pepper; set aside. Melt butter in a skillet over medium heat. Saute onion, ham and green pepper for 4 to 5 minutes. Spoon ham mixture into a greased 8"x8" casserole dish or 4 small ramekins. Pour egg mixture over ham mixture. Sprinkle with cheese. Bake, uncovered at 350 degrees for 20 to 25 minutes, until eggs are set. Serve topped with a dollop of sour cream and chopped chives.

Kristi Vandenham, Fillmore, CA

Quick Bacon & Potato Tart

This is delicious with whatever cheese you have on hand.

Makes 6 servings

1 T. butter
1 lb. bacon
1-1/2 lbs. potatoes, peeled, sliced and divided
1-1/4 c. shredded Cheddar cheese, divided
salt and pepper to taste

Spread butter in an 8" round baking pan; place bacon over butter, arranging in spoke-like fashion. Bring bacon up the sides and over the edge of the pan. Top with half the potatoes; sprinkle with half the cheese. Layer with remaining potatoes and cheese; top with salt and pepper. Fold ends of bacon slices across the top; bake at 400 degrees for about one hour, or until potatoes are tender.

★ TIME-SAVER ★ Bake a family-favorite omelet or quiche in muffin cups or ramekins for individual servings in a jiffy. When making minis, reduce the baking time by about 10 minutes, and test for doneness with a toothpick.

Quick & Easy Cheesy Baked Omelet

Anne Muns, Scottsdale, AZ

Garden-Fresh Egg Casserole

Make this casserole the night before you'll be serving it. You'll have more time to spend with family & friends!

Serves 8 to 10

1 c. buttermilk
1/2 c. onion, grated
1-1/2 c. shredded Monterey Jack
  cheese
1 c. cottage cheese
1 c. spinach, chopped
1 c. tomatoes, chopped
1/2 c. butter, melted
18 eggs, beaten

Mix all ingredients together; pour into a greased 13"x9" baking pan. Cover; refrigerate overnight. Bake at 350 degrees for 50 minutes to one hour.

Terri Scungio, Williamsburg, VA

Spinach Quiche

Even if your kids say they don't like spinach, they will love this quiche!

Makes 8 servings

12-oz. pkg. frozen spinach soufflé,
  thawed
2 eggs, beaten
3 T. 2% milk
2 t. onion, chopped
3/4 c. Italian ground pork sausage,
  browned and drained
1/2 c. sliced mushrooms
3/4 c. low-fat shredded Swiss cheese
9-inch pie crust, baked

In a bowl, mix together all ingredients except crust; pour into crust. Bake at 400 degrees for 30 to 45 minutes, until golden and center is set. Cut into wedges.

★ SAVVY SWAP ★ For a fresh change from spinach, give Swiss chard a try. An old-timey favorite that probably grew in your grandmother's garden, it's easy to serve too...just steam until tender, then drizzle with cider vinegar to taste.

Garden-Fresh Egg Casserole

Chip Woods, Worthington, OH

Chocolate-Chip Oven Pancake

I made this for my boys when they were growing up. Now they make this for their own children!

Makes 4 servings

3 eggs, beaten
1/2 c. milk
1/2 c. all-purpose flour
1/4 t. salt
1/2 c. chocolate chips
1 T. butter, melted
Garnish: chocolate chips, pancake syrup

In a bowl, whisk together eggs, milk, flour and salt until smooth. Stir in chocolate chips. Spread butter in a 9" pie plate; add batter. Bake at 400 degrees for about 20 minutes, until cooked through. Serve topped with additional chocolate chips and pancake syrup.

Hannah Hilgendorf, Nashotah, WI

Peachy Baked Oatmeal

We use fresh peaches when they are in season. There's nothing better!

Makes 6 servings

2 eggs, beaten
1/2 c. brown sugar, packed
1-1/2 t. baking powder
1/4 t. salt
1-1/2 t. cinnamon
1/2 t. nutmeg
1-1/2 t. vanilla extract
3/4 c. milk
3 c. long-cooking oats, uncooked
1/3 c. oil
16-oz. can sliced peaches, partially drained
Garnish: warm milk

In a bowl, combine eggs, brown sugar, baking powder, salt, spices and vanilla; beat well. Add remaining ingredients except garnish; mix thoroughly. Spoon into a greased 8"x8" baking pan. Bake at 375 degrees for 20 to 25 minutes, until center is set. Serve in bowls, topped with warm milk.

Chocolate-Chip Oven Pancake

Caroline Macey, Chicago, IL

Quick & Easy Quiche

Purchased pie crusts make quiche-making so easy!

Serves 6 to 8

1/2 of a 2.8-oz pkg. cooked bacon
9-inch pie crust
8 eggs
8-oz jar creamy blue cheese salad
    dressing
1 T. fresh parsley, chopped
Garnish: fresh chives

Crumble bacon into pie crust. Blend together eggs, salad dressing and parsley in a large bowl; pour into crust. Bake at 350 degrees for 25 to 30 minutes, or until puffed and a knife inserted in the center comes out clean. Cool on a wire rack for 5 minutes before cutting.

Natasha Morris, Ulysses, KS

Egg Casserole Deluxe

This recipe is so versatile! My youngest daughter made this for her sister's bridal shower...it was a big hit with the bride-to-be and the guests! For a crowd, simply double the recipe and bake in a 13"x9" baking pan. For a quick weeknight dinner, just add a fruit salad and dinner is done!

Makes 8 servings

1 to 2 T. butter
1/2 cup sliced mushrooms
1 doz. eggs, beaten
8-oz. container sour cream
1/2 c. shredded Cheddar cheese
2.8-oz. pkg. pre-cooked bacon,
    crumbled and divided

Melt butter in a large skillet over medium heat. Sauté mushrooms. Add eggs; cook and stir until softly scrambled. Stir in sour cream, mushrooms, cheese and half of bacon. Transfer to a lightly greased 8"x8" baking pan. Sprinkle remaining bacon on top. Bake, uncovered, at 350 degrees for 30 minutes.

Quick & Easy Quiche

Jo Ann, Gooseberry Patch

Strawberry-Banana Baked Pancake

Sometimes we use fresh blueberries or raspberries for this recipe. They are all tasty!

Makes 4 servings

1/3 c. butter
1 c. flour
1 c. milk
4 eggs, beaten
2 t. sugar
1/2 t. salt
1 banana, sliced
1 c. strawberries, sliced
1 T. lemon juice
Garnish: powdered sugar

Place butter in a 9" pie plate; place pan in oven to melt butter while preparing filling. In a bowl, whisk together flour, milk, eggs, sugar and salt. Pour mixture into melted butter in pan. Bake, uncovered, at 425 degrees for 20 to 25 minutes, until pancake is golden and center is set. In a small bowl, toss banana and strawberries with lemon juice. Spoon fruit over warm pancake. Garnish with powdered sugar.

Carol Lytle, Columbus, OH

Blackberry Buckle

We love to serve this coffee cake for special breakfasts or on the weekends.

Makes 9 servings

2 c. all-purpose flour
2-1/2 t. baking powder
1/4 t. salt
1/2 c. butter
3/4 c. sugar
1 egg, beaten
1/2 c. milk
2 c. blackberries

Stir together flour, baking powder and salt; set aside. In a separate bowl, blend butter and sugar until light and fluffy. Add egg and beat well. Add flour mixture and milk alternately to egg mixture, beating until smooth. Pour into a greased 9"x9" baking pan; top with blackberries and Crumb Topping. Bake at 350 degrees for 50 to 60 minutes, until golden. Serve warm.

Crumb Topping:

1/2 c. all-purpose flour
1/2 c. sugar
1/2 t. cinnamon
1/4 c. butter

Sift together flour, sugar and cinnamon. Cut in butter until mixture resembles coarse crumbs.

Strawberry-Banana Baked Pancake

Wendy Jacobs, Idaho Falls, ID

Potato & Onion Frittata

Make a hearty, warm breakfast using a little leftover ham and potato from last night's dinner.

Makes 4 servings

2 to 3 T. olive oil, divided
1 yellow onion, peeled and thinly
    sliced
1/4 c. cooked ham, diced
1 c. potatoes, peeled, cooked and diced
4 eggs, beaten
1/3 c. shredded Parmesan cheese
salt to taste

Heat 2 tablespoons oil over medium heat in a non-stick skillet. Add onion; cook and stir for 2 to 3 minutes. Add ham and potatoes. Cook until onion and potatoes are lightly golden. With a slotted spoon, remove mixture to a bowl; cool slightly. Stir eggs, cheese and salt into onion mixture. Return skillet to medium heat; add the remaining oil, if needed. When skillet is hot, add onion mixture. Cook until frittata is golden on the bottom and top begins to set, about 4 to 5 minutes. Place a plate over skillet and carefully invert frittata onto the plate. Slide frittata back into skillet. Cook until bottom is lightly golden, 2 to 3 minutes. Cut into wedges; serve warm or at room temperature.

Nadine Watson, Aurora, CO

Mexican Egg Bake

Refried beans make a perfect side for this dish.

Serves 8 to 10

12 corn tortillas, torn
16-oz. can green chili sauce
16-oz. pkg. shredded Cheddar
    cheese, divided
6 eggs
Garnish: sour cream, shredded
    lettuce and chopped tomato

Layer tortillas, chili sauce and 3/4 of cheese in an ungreased 13"x9" baking pan. Break eggs over top, spacing evenly. Sprinkle with remaining cheese. Bake, uncovered, at 350 degrees for 30 to 40 minutes. Slice into squares and garnish with sour cream, lettuce and tomato.

★ SIMPLE SIDE ★ Omelets and frittatas are perfect for using up all kinds of odds & ends from the fridge. Mushrooms, tomatoes and asparagus are especially good with eggs. Slice or dice veggies and sauté until tender... scrumptious!

Potato & Onion Frittata

Nelda Columbo, Port Arthur, TX

Strawberry French Toast

We share this special breakfast when the grandchildren visit. Depending on the size of your bread loaf, you might need to use less milk.

Serves 4 to 8

1 uncut loaf French bread
8-oz. pkg. cream cheese, softened
10-oz. jar strawberry jam
6 eggs, beaten
4-1/2 c. milk
1/2 to 1 c. sugar, to taste
Optional: powdered sugar

Slice bread crossways in one-inch slices, without cutting through bottom crust. Slice once down the center lengthwise, again without cutting through bottom crust. Place loaf in a buttered 13"x9" baking pan. Spread cream cheese over top of loaf; spread jam over cheese and set aside. In a bowl, beat together eggs, milk and sugar; pour over loaf. Cover with foil and refrigerate overnight. Bake, covered, at 350 degrees for 45 minutes. Uncover and bake for 15 minutes more. Cut slices apart for serving; sprinkle with powdered sugar, if desired.

Lori Hurley, Fishers, IN

French Toast Casserole

A really simple way to make French toast for a crowd. Pop it in the fridge the night before, then all you have to do is bake it the next day. Serve with bacon for a great dinner!

Serves 6 to 8

1 c. brown sugar, packed
1/2 c. butter
2 c. corn syrup
1 loaf French bread, sliced
5 eggs, beaten
1-1/2 c. milk
Garnish: powdered sugar, maple syrup

Melt together brown sugar, butter and corn syrup in a saucepan over low heat; pour into a greased 13"x9" baking pan. Arrange bread slices over mixture and set aside. Whisk together eggs and milk; pour over bread, coating all slices. Cover and refrigerate overnight. Uncover and bake at 350 degrees for 30 minutes, or until lightly golden. Sprinkle with powdered sugar; serve with warm syrup.

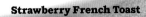
Strawberry French Toast

Kathy Grashoff, Fort Wayne, IN

Blueberry & Cream Cheese Strata

This berry-filled strata is just right for a leisurely breakfast with family & friends.

Serves 4 to 6

16-oz. loaf white bread, crusts
   removed, cubed and divided
2 c. frozen blueberries, divided
3-oz. pkg. cream cheese, cut into
   1/4-inch cubes
4 eggs, beaten
2 c. milk
1/3 c. sugar
1 t. vanilla extract
1/4 t. salt
1/4 t. nutmeg

Place half of the bread in a greased 8"x8" baking pan; top with half of the blueberries. Top with cream cheese, remaining bread and remaining blueberries; set aside. Beat eggs, milk, sugar, vanilla, salt and nutmeg with an electric mixer on medium speed until blended. Pour over bread mixture and refrigerate for 20 minutes to overnight. Bake, uncovered, at 325 degrees for one hour.

Athena Colegrove, Big Springs, TX

Sweetie Banana Oatmeal

My little ones, with Daddy's help, made this for me on Valentine's Day... what a yummy breakfast surprise from my 3 sweeties!

Makes 4 servings

2 c. long-cooking oats, uncooked
1/2 c. sweetened condensed milk
4 c. water
2 bananas, thinly sliced

Combine oats, milk and water in a slow cooker that has been sprayed with non-stick vegetable spray. Cover and cook on low setting for 6 to 8 hours. Add bananas 10 to 15 minutes before serving.

★ **FREEZE IT** ★ So the produce counter had a wonderful sale and now you wonder what to do with 5 pounds of blueberries. Don't fret...it's easy to freeze fresh berries for later! Simply place the berries in a single layer on a baking sheet, freeze, then store in plastic freezer bags.

Blueberry & Cream Cheese Strata

Cherylann Smith, Efland, NC

Herbed Sausage Quiche

Serve this quiche right from the table... it is so pretty!

Makes 8 servings

9-inch frozen pie crust, thawed
1 c. ground pork breakfast sausage, browned and drained
3 eggs, beaten
1 c. 2 % milk
1 c. low-fat shredded Cheddar cheese
1 sprig fresh rosemary, chopped
1-1/2 t. Italian seasoning
1/4 t. salt
1/4 t. pepper

Bake pie crust according to package directions. Mix together remaining ingredients in a bowl; spread into baked crust. Bake, uncovered, at 450 degrees for 15 minutes. Reduce oven temperature to 350 degrees, cover with foil and bake 9 more minutes. Cut into wedges to serve.

Stacie Avner, Delaware, OH

Crab, Corn & Pepper Frittata

When it is in season, use fresh corn.

Serves 4 to 6

6 eggs, beaten
1/3 c. corn
1/3 c. mayonnaise
1/4 c. milk
2 T. green onions, chopped
2 T. red pepper, chopped
salt and pepper to taste
1 c. crabmeat, flaked
1 c. shredded Monterey Jack cheese
Garnish: chopped green onions

Whisk together eggs, corn, mayonnaise, milk, onions, red pepper and salt and pepper to taste. Gently stir in crabmeat. Pour into a greased 10" pie plate. Bake at 350 degrees for 15 to 20 minutes. Sprinkle with cheese and bake for 5 more minutes, or until cheese is melted. Garnish with green onions.

Herbed Sausage Quiche

Georgia Cooper, Helena, MT

Ham-and-Tomato Pie

Summer's best flavors are blended in this quiche-style recipe...sweet fresh basil, juicy plum tomatoes and crisp green onions.

Makes 6 servings

8-oz. pkg. cooked ham, diced
1/2 c. green onions, sliced
9-inch frozen pie crust, thawed
1 T. Dijon mustard
1 c. shredded mozzarella cheese, divided
2 plum tomatoes, thinly sliced
1 egg
1/3 c. half-and-half
1 T. fresh basil, chopped
1/8 t. pepper

Sauté ham and green onions in a large non-stick skillet over medium heat 5 minutes, or until ham is browned and any liquid evaporates. Brush bottom of pie crust evenly with mustard; sprinkle with 1/2 cup mozzarella cheese. Spoon ham mixture evenly over cheese and top with sliced tomatoes arranged in a single layer. Beat egg and half-and-half with a fork until blended; pour over tomatoes. Sprinkle evenly with basil, pepper and remaining 1/2 cup cheese. Bake on lowest oven rack at 425 degrees for 20 to 23 minutes, until lightly golden and set. Cool on a wire rack 20 minutes. Cut into wedges to serve.

★ JUICY TIP ★ Apples speed ripening of peaches, pears, tomatoes, and avocados when stored together in a brown bag. Set in a warm dark place and punch a few holes in the bag for ventilation.

Ham-and-Tomato Pie

Turkey Day Leftovers Casserole, Page 92

CHAPTER THREE

Simple Suppers

Zesty Italian Chicken, Page 114

Country Chicken Pot Pie, Page 126

Marie Buche, Yakima, WA

Hamburger Pie

With a family of six on a ministry budget, this easy, affordable recipe became the first dinner I taught my three daughters and my son to prepare. Even the leftovers are tasty. This is also my most-requested church potluck recipe. Serve with cinnamon-spiced applesauce for a wonderful family dinner.

Makes 12 servings

2 lbs. ground beef
1 onion, chopped
2 10-3/4 oz. cans tomato soup
28-oz. can green beans, drained
salt and pepper to taste
1 c. shredded Cheddar cheese

Brown beef and onion together in a skillet; drain. Mix soup and beans in a lightly greased 13"x9" baking pan. Stir in beef mixture, salt and pepper; set aside. Spread Potato Topping evenly over mixture in pan; sprinkle with cheese. Bake, uncovered, at 350 degrees for about 30 minutes.

Potato Topping:

3 c. milk
3 c. water
1/4 c. margarine
1 t. salt
4 c. instant mashed potato flakes

Bring all ingredients except potato flakes to a boil. Stir in potato flakes; mix well. Cover and let stand for 5 minutes. If potatoes are too thick to spread, add milk or water to desired consistency.

Jennifer Williams, Los Angeles, CA

Cheeseburger Bake

This hearty meal is great after a long day of work and errands...so filling.

Makes 4 servings

8-oz. tube refrigerated crescent rolls
1 lb. ground beef
1-1/4 oz. pkg. taco seasoning
15-oz. can tomato sauce
2 c. shredded Cheddar cheese

Unroll crescent roll dough; press into a greased 9" round baking pan, pinching seams closed. Bake at 350 degrees for 10 minutes; set aside. Meanwhile, brown beef in a skillet over medium heat; drain. Add taco seasoning and sauce; heat through. Spoon over crescent rolls and sprinkle cheese on top. Bake, uncovered, for 10 to 15 minutes. Let stand 5 minutes before serving.

★ FLAVOR BURST ★ A sprinkle of herbs can really perk up the flavor of casseroles. Some good choices are parsley, basil, oregano and thyme.

Hamburger Pie

Brenda Hager, Nancy, KY

Sourdough Chicken Casserole

My husband really enjoys this delicious dish, and he's not a big fan of chicken. The caramelized onions give it a great flavor!

Makes 4 servings

4 c. sourdough bread, cubed
6 T. butter, melted and divided
1/3 c. grated Parmesan cheese
2 T. fresh parsley, chopped
2 sweet onions, sliced
8-oz. pkg. sliced mushrooms
10-3/4 oz. can cream of
    mushroom soup
1 c. white wine or buttermilk
2-1/2 c. cooked chicken, shredded
1/2 c. roasted red peppers,
    drained and chopped
1/2 t. salt
1/4 t. pepper

Toss together bread cubes, 1/4 cup butter, cheese and parsley in a large bowl; set aside. Sauté onions in remaining 2 tablespoons butter in a large skillet over medium-high heat 15 minutes, or until dark golden. Add mushrooms and sauté 5 minutes. Add remaining ingredients. Cook 5 more minutes, stirring constantly, until hot and bubbly. Pour into 4 lightly greased ramekins; top each ramekin with bread cube mixture. Bake, uncovered, at 400 degrees for 15 minutes, or until golden.

Jo Ann, Gooseberry Patch

Party Paella Casserole

Here's a great use for rotisserie chicken, shrimp and yellow rice. We like to serve this on New Year's Eve or at our Super Bowl party.

Serves 8

2 8-oz. pkgs. yellow rice, uncooked
1 lb. medium shrimp, cleaned
1 T. fresh lemon juice
1/2 t. salt
1/4 t. pepper
2 cloves garlic, minced
1-1/2 T. olive oil
2-1/2 lb. lemon & garlic deli rotisserie
    chicken, coarsely shredded
5 green onions, chopped
8-oz. container sour cream
1 c. frozen English peas, thawed
1 c. green olives with pimentos,
    coarsely chopped
1-1/2 c. shredded Monterey Jack cheese
1/2 t. smoked Spanish paprika

Prepare rice according to package directions. Remove from heat and let cool 30 minutes; fluff with a fork. Meanwhile, toss shrimp with lemon juice, salt and pepper in a bowl. Sauté seasoned shrimp and garlic in hot oil in a large non-stick skillet 2 minutes or just until done. Remove from heat. Combine shredded chicken, rice, green onions, sour cream and peas in a large bowl; toss well. Add shrimp and olives, tossing gently. Spoon rice mixture into a greased 13"x9" baking pan. Combine cheese and paprika, tossing well; sprinkle over casserole. Bake, uncovered, at 400 degrees for 15 minutes or just until cheese is melted and casserole is thoroughly heated.

Sourdough Chicken Casserole

Penny Sherman, Cumming, GA

South-of-the-Border Chicken

Scrumptious...makes any meal a fiesta!

Makes 4 servings

2 T. all-purpose flour
14-1/2 oz. can diced tomatoes with
   chili seasoning
2 t. diced jalapeños
1/2 t. salt
15-oz. can black beans, drained and
   rinsed
6 boneless, skinless chicken breasts
1 yellow pepper, sliced

Shake flour in a large oven bag;
place bag in a 13"x9" baking pan. Add
tomatoes, jalapeños and salt to bag;
squeeze to blend with flour. Add beans
and chicken to bag; turn to coat
chicken. Top with yellow pepper.
Close bag with nylon tie provided;
cut six, 1/2-inch slits in top. Bake at
350 degrees for 45 to 50 minutes,
until chicken juices run clear.

Carrie Knotts, Kalispell, MT

Spicy Sausage & Chicken Creole

I used this dish to win over my husband
and his family while we were dating. He
likes his food spicy! Of course, you can
use a little less hot pepper sauce if
you prefer.

Makes 4 servings

14-1/2 oz. can chopped tomatoes
1/2 c. long-cooking rice, uncooked
1/2 c. hot water
2 t. hot pepper sauce
1/4 t. garlic powder
1/4 t. dried oregano
16-oz. pkg. frozen broccoli, corn & red
   pepper blend, thawed
4 boneless, skinless chicken thighs
1/2 lb. link Italian pork sausage,
   cooked and quartered
8-oz. can tomato sauce

Combine tomatoes, rice, water, hot
sauce and seasonings in a 13"x9" baking
pan. Cover and bake at 375 degrees for
10 minutes. Stir vegetables into tomato
mixture; top with chicken and sausage.
Pour tomato sauce over top. Bake,
covered, at 375 degrees for 40 minutes,
or until juices of chicken run clear.

South-of-the-Border Chicken

Valerie Neeley, Robinson, IL

Zesty Pizza Casserole

Add your favorite pizza toppings to this easy casserole.

Serves 4 to 6

1 lb. ground beef
1/2 c. onion, chopped
1/2 c. green pepper, chopped
2 c. cooked elbow macaroni
2 15-oz. cans pizza sauce
4-oz. can sliced mushrooms, drained
4-oz. pkg. sliced pepperoni
1/2 t. dried oregano
1/2 t. garlic powder
1/2 t. dried basil
1/2 t. salt
3/4 c. shredded mozzarella cheese
Garnish: sliced fresh basil

Brown beef with onion and green pepper in a large skillet over medium heat. Drain; stir in remaining ingredients except cheese and garnish. Transfer to a lightly greased 2-quart casserole dish; sprinkle with cheese. Bake, uncovered, at 350 degrees for 30 to 45 minutes, until hot and bubbly. Garnish with basil.

Vickie, Gooseberry Patch

Pepperoni & Cheese Quiche

This pizza-like, no-shell quiche will be a favorite for the entire family. Make 2 and freeze one for later.

Serves 3 to 4

2 eggs, beaten
3/4 c. all-purpose flour
1 c. milk
1/2 t. salt
1/8 t. pepper
1/2 c. Muenster cheese, shredded
1/2 c. shredded Cheddar cheese
1/4 c. pepperoni, finely chopped

Whisk together first 5 ingredients. Stir in cheeses and pepperoni. Pour into an ungreased 8" pie plate; bake at 375 degrees for 30 minutes, or until puffy and golden.

★ TASTY TIP ★ For a tasty change, make a quick, savory crumb crust for a quiche. Spread 2-1/2 tablespoons softened butter in a pie plate, then firmly press 2-1/2 cups seasoned dry bread crumbs or cracker crumbs into the butter. Freeze until firm, pour in filling and bake as directed.

Zesty Pizza Casserole

Jeff Howell, Minonk, IL

Turkey Day Leftovers Casserole

I came up with this the day after Thanksgiving when we had lots of leftovers. Add a dish of cranberry sauce on the side.

Serves 6 to 8

3 c. cooked stuffing, or 6-oz.
   pkg. chicken stuffing mix,
   prepared
2 to 3 c. cooked turkey, chopped
   or shredded
1-1/2 to 2 c. turkey gravy
2 c. green bean casserole or
   cooked green beans
4 c. mashed potatoes
2 eggs, beaten
1/4 c. milk
1 c. biscuit baking mix
Garnish: shredded Swiss cheese

Spread stuffing evenly in a 13"x9" baking pan sprayed with non-stick vegetable spray. Layer turkey over stuffing; spoon gravy over turkey. Layer with green beans and mashed potatoes; set aside. In a bowl, stir together eggs, milk and biscuit mix; spread batter evenly over potatoes. Sprinkle with cheese. Bake, uncovered, at 400 degrees for 30 to 35 minutes, until hot and cheese is melted.

Shirley Gist, Zanesville, OH

Turkey Tetrazzini

This yummy casserole is our family's favorite way to enjoy leftover holiday turkey. It's easy to toss together, too.

Makes 6 servings

8-oz. pkg. thin spaghetti, uncooked
2 cubes chicken bouillon
2 to 3 T. dried, minced onion
2 10-3/4 oz. cans cream of mushroom
   soup
8-oz. container sour cream
1/2 c. milk
salt and pepper to taste
2 c. cooked turkey, cubed
8-oz. can sliced mushrooms, drained
8-oz. pkg. shredded Cheddar cheese

Cook spaghetti according to package directions, adding bouillon and onion to cooking water. Drain and place in a large bowl. Stir together soup, sour cream, milk, salt and pepper in a medium bowl; fold in turkey and mushrooms. Lightly stir mixture into spaghetti, coating well. Pour into a lightly greased 13"x9" baking pan; top with cheese. Bake at 350 degrees for 30 to 40 minutes, until hot and bubbly.

Turkey Day Leftovers Casserole

Tina Wright, Atlanta, GA

One-Dish Tuna & Noodles

This is one of those simple dishes we all remember from childhood. Make this on a Sunday afternoon and freeze it for later in the week!

Serves 4 to 6

1 c. egg noodles, uncooked
10-3/4 oz. can cream of mushroom soup
2/3 c. water
2 t. chopped pimentos
1 c. American cheese, chopped
7-oz. can tuna, drained

Cook noodles according to package directions; drain. Meanwhile, combine soup and water in a saucepan over medium heat. Cook until smooth, stirring frequently. Fold in pimentos and cheese; stir until cheese melts. Remove from heat and set aside. Combine tuna and noodles in a bowl and mix well; spoon into a lightly greased shallow 2-quart casserole dish. Pour cheese mixture on top; stir gently to mix. Bake, uncovered, at 375 degrees for 30 minutes, until hot and bubbly.

Kimberly Lyons, Commerce, TX

Chicken & Rice Casserole

Great with fresh-baked bread and a green salad.

Serves 6 to 8

2 6.2-oz. pkgs. quick-cooking long-grain and wild rice with seasoning packets
4 boneless, skinless chicken breasts, cooked and cut into 1" cubes
3 10-3/4 oz. cans cream of mushroom soup
1-1/3 c. frozen mixed vegetables, thawed
3 c. water

Gently stir together all ingredients. Spread into an ungreased 13"x9" baking pan. Bake, uncovered, at 350 degrees about 45 minutes, stirring occasionally.

★ SIMPLE SWAP ★ Ingredient swaps are easy with most casserole recipes. If there's no cream of mushroom soup in the pantry, cream of celery or chicken is sure to be just as tasty...you may even discover a new way you like even better!

One-Dish Tuna & Noodles

Kerry Mayer, Dunham Springs, LA

Western Pork Chops

For a delicious variation, try substituting peeled, cubed sweet potatoes for the redskins.

Makes 4 servings

1 T. all-purpose flour
1 c. barbecue sauce
4 pork chops
salt and pepper to taste
4 redskin potatoes, sliced
1 green pepper, cubed
1 c. baby carrots

Shake flour in a large, plastic zipping bag. Add barbecue sauce to bag and squeeze bag to blend in flour. Season pork chops with salt and pepper; add pork chops to bag. Turn bag to coat pork chops with sauce. On a baking sheet, arrange vegetables in an even layer. Remove pork chops from bag and place on top of vegetables. Cover with foil making a slit on the top. Bake at 350 degrees for about 40 to 45 minutes, until pork chops and vegetables are tender.

Robin Kessler, Fresno, CA

Oodles of Noodles Chili Bake

Create a different dish by adding your favorite vegetables. It's foolproof and delicious either way!

Makes 4 servings

12-oz. pkg. wide egg noodles, uncooked
1 lb. ground beef
14-1/2 oz. can diced tomatoes
15-oz. can corn, drained
15-oz. can chili
1 c. shredded Cheddar cheese, divided

Cook noodles according to package directions; drain and set aside. Meanwhile, brown beef in a skillet over medium heat; drain. Combine tomatoes with juice and remaining ingredients except 1/4 cup cheese in a lightly greased 13"x9" baking pan. Top with remaining cheese. Bake, uncovered, at 350 degrees for about 20 minutes, or until heated through.

★ EASY SOLUTION ★ Out of diced tomatoes in your pantry? Use a pair of clean kitchen shears to cut canned whole tomatoes while they're still in the can. So easy!

Western Pork Chops

Betty Lou Wright, Hendersonville, TN

Top-Prize Chicken Casserole

This crowd-pleasing dish has graced my family's table for decades. Originally prepared by my mother-in-law, it's been taken to many potlucks and church suppers. With its creamy sauce and crunchy topping, it's always a hit.

Serves 6 to 8

2 to 3 c. cooked chicken, cubed
2 10-3/4 oz. cans cream of
    mushroom soup
4 eggs, hard-boiled, peeled and
    chopped
1 onion, chopped
2 c. cooked rice
1-1/2 c. celery, chopped
1 c. mayonnaise
2 T. lemon juice
3-oz. pkg. slivered almonds
5-oz. can chow mein noodles

Combine all ingredients except almonds and noodles in a large bowl; mix well. Transfer mixture to a lightly greased 3-quart casserole dish. Cover and refrigerate 8 hours to overnight. Stir in almonds. Bake, uncovered, at 350 degrees for 40 to 45 minutes, until heated through. Top with noodles; bake 5 more minutes.

Sandy Rowe, Bellevue, OH

Pot Roast Casserole

Any type of pasta works in this recipe...even rotini!

Makes 4 servings

8-oz. pkg. fine egg noodles, cooked
2 c. beef pot roast, cooked and
    chopped
2 c. Alfredo sauce
1 c. sliced mushrooms
1/4 c. dry bread crumbs

Mix noodles, pot roast, Alfredo sauce and mushrooms in an ungreased 2-quart casserole dish; sprinkle with bread crumbs. Bake at 350 degrees for 20 to 30 minutes, until crumbs are golden.

★ CRISPY TIP ★ **Try a new topping on a tried & true casserole...sprinkle on seasoned dry bread crumbs, flavored snack cracker crumbs or crispy chow mein noodles. To keep the topping crisp, leave the casserole dish uncovered while it bakes.**

Top-Prize Chicken Casserole

Britni Rexwinkle, Green Forest, AR

Upside-Down Mexican Pot Pie

This is the first recipe my husband and I came up with together in college...we just tossed together some things we had on hand. It was a keeper! Sometimes I substitute shredded chicken.

Makes 6 servings

1 lb. ground beef
1 onion, chopped
1 green pepper, chopped
1 zucchini, chopped
4-oz. can diced green chiles
14-1/2 oz. can diced tomatoes
11-oz. can corn, drained
8-1/2 oz. pkg. cornbread mix
1 c. shredded Mexican-blend cheese

In a skillet over medium-high heat, brown beef with onion, green pepper, zucchini and chiles; drain. Add tomatoes with juice and corn; simmer for about 5 minutes. Meanwhile, prepare cornbread mix according to package directions; pour batter into a lightly greased 2-quart casserole dish. Spoon beef mixture over batter; sprinkle with cheese. Bake, covered with aluminum foil, at 350 degrees for 25 minutes. Uncover; bake an additional 5 minutes, or until cheese is melted.

★ SWEET REWARD ★ Serve up some "fried" ice cream with a Mexican feast. Freeze scoops of ice cream, roll in crushed frosted corn flake cereal and drizzle with honey. Top with cinnamon, whipped cream and a cherry. Yum!

Upside-Down Mexican Pot Pie

SIMPLE SUPPERS

Margaret Vinci, Pasadena, CA

Momma's Divine Divan

Choose rotisserie chicken from your supermarket deli to add more flavor to this family favorite. Generally, one rotisserie chicken will yield 3 cups of chopped meat, so you'll need 2 rotisserie chickens to get the 4 to 5 cups needed for this recipe. Add cooked rice, and you have a complete meal!

Serves 8 to 10

1/2 lb. broccoli flowerets, cooked
4 to 5 boneless, skinless chicken
   breasts, cooked and cubed
salt to taste
1 c. seasoned dry bread crumbs
1 T. butter, melted
10-3/4 oz. can cream of chicken
   soup
1/2 c. mayonnaise
1 t. curry powder
1/2 t. lemon juice
1 c. shredded Cheddar cheese

Arrange broccoli in a lightly greased 13"x9" baking pan. Sprinkle chicken with salt to taste; place on top of broccoli and set aside. Toss together bread crumbs and butter; set aside. Combine soup, mayonnaise, curry powder and lemon juice in a separate bowl; spread over chicken and broccoli. Top with cheese; sprinkle with bread crumb mixture. Bake, uncovered, at 350 degrees for 25 minutes, or until hot and bubbly.

Dorothy Benson, Baton Rouge, LA

Chicken Spaghetti Deluxe

This recipe is reminiscent of cold winter days and the inviting smells of Mom's warm kitchen. Best of all, the pasta doesn't need to be cooked ahead of time.

Makes 8 servings

2 c. cooked chicken, chopped
8-oz. pkg. spaghetti, uncooked and
   broken into 2-inch pieces
1 c. celery, chopped
1 c. onion, chopped
1 c. yellow pepper, chopped
1 c. red pepper, chopped
2 10-3/4 oz. cans cream of
   mushroom soup
1 c. chicken broth
1/4 t. Cajun seasoning or pepper
1 c. shredded Cheddar cheese

Mix chicken, spaghetti, celery, onion, yellow pepper and red pepper in a bowl. Whisk together soup, broth and seasoning in a separate bowl. Add chicken mixture to soup mixture. Spread chicken mixture in a lightly greased 13"x9" baking pan; sprinkle cheese over top. Cover with aluminum foil coated with non-stick vegetable spray. Bake at 350 degrees for 45 minutes. Uncover and bake for 10 more minutes.

Momma's Divine Divan

Becky Holsinger, Belpre, OH

Easy Chicken Manicotti

Although I love to cook, I don't claim to be all that great at it. I was given this recipe when I got married and not only is it easy, it tastes great! I know when I make this dish it will be good, no matter what.

Serves 5 to 7

26-oz. jar pasta sauce
1/2 c. water
10 boneless, skinless chicken tenders
1 t. garlic salt
1/2 t. Italian seasoning
10 manicotti pasta shells, uncooked
8-oz. pkg. shredded mozzarella
　cheese
Optional: chopped fresh basil and
　oregano

In a bowl, mix pasta sauce and water. Spread 1/3 of sauce mixture in an ungreased 13"x9" glass baking pan; set aside. Sprinkle chicken with seasonings. Insert one chicken tender into each uncooked manicotti shell, stuffing from each end, if necessary. Arrange shells over sauce mixture in baking pan. Pour remaining sauce mixture evenly over shells, covering completely. Cover with aluminum foil. Bake at 350 degrees for about one hour, until shells are tender and chicken is no longer pink in the center. Top with cheese. Bake, uncovered, for 5 minutes, or until cheese is melted. Garnish with herbs, if desired.

★ HEALTHY HABIT ★ Try serving a meatless main once a week...it's economical and healthy too. Cheese-filled manicotti with tomato sauce can stand alone as the main course. Fill manicotti in minutes by using your cookie press...just pack with cheese filling and squeeze. Pastry bags work just as well too.

Easy Chicken Manicotti

Alma Meyers, Guernsey, WY

Quick Salisbury Steak

Add a side of mashed potatoes for a hearty, filling dinner.

Makes 4 servings

1 lb. ground beef
1-1/2 oz. pkg. onion soup mix
2 eggs, beaten
2 10-3/4 oz. cans golden mushroom
  soup

In a large bowl, combine beef, soup mix and eggs; mix well and form into 4 patties. Place patties in an ungreased 13"x9" baking pan; cover with soup. Bake at 350 degrees for 35 minutes, or until patties are no longer pink in the center.

Tabetha Moore, New Braunfels, TX

Super-Easy Stuffed Peppers

My husband says these are the best peppers!

Makes 4 servings

4 green, red or orange peppers, tops
  removed
1 lb. ground beef
1 onion, diced
1 T. Italian seasoning
1 clove garlic, pressed
3 c. cooked brown rice
26-oz. can spaghetti sauce, divided
salt and pepper to taste
Garnish: shredded Parmesan cheese

Bring a large saucepan of water to a boil; add peppers and boil until tender. Drain and set aside. Brown ground beef with onion in a skillet; drain. Add Italian seasoning and garlic. Set aside 1/2 cup spaghetti sauce. Combine ground beef mixture, remaining sauce, cooked rice, salt and pepper in a bowl. Arrange peppers in a lightly greased 8"x8" baking pan. Fill peppers completely with ground beef mixture, spooning any extra mixture between peppers. Top with reserved sauce. Add pepper tops if using. Lightly cover with aluminum foil; bake at 400 degrees for 20 to 25 minutes. Sprinkle with Parmesan cheese.

Quick Salisbury Steak

Missy Pluta, Portage, MI

Puffy Potato Casserole

Scatter French fried onions on top for a crunchy garnish.

Serves 4 to 6

1 lb. ground beef, browned and drained
10-3/4 oz. can cream of mushroom
   soup
10-3/4 oz. can cream of chicken soup
2 14-1/2 oz. cans green beans, drained
8 slices American cheese
32-oz. pkg. frozen potato puffs

Spoon ground beef into a 13"x9" baking pan; top with soups. Layer green beans over soups; arrange cheese slices on top. Top with a single layer of potato puffs. Bake at 350 degrees for 30 to 40 minutes.

Sheryl Eastman, Wixom, MI

Sausage & Apple Kraut

Serve with mashed potatoes, buttered green beans and fresh-baked rolls for a satisfying chilly-weather meal.

Serves 4 to 6

27-oz. jar sauerkraut, drained, rinsed
   and divided
1 lb. Kielbasa sausage, sliced and
   divided
2 tart apples, peeled, cored and diced
1/2 c. brown sugar, packed and divided
2 c. apple cider or juice, divided

In a lightly greased 13"x9" baking pan, layer half of sauerkraut, half of sausage and all the apples. Sprinkle with 1/4 cup brown sugar. Pour one cup cider or juice over top. Repeat layering. Cover and bake at 350 degrees for 1-1/2 hours, or until sauerkraut is caramelized and golden.

Puffy Potato Casserole

Myra Barker, Gap, PA

Cheesy Chicken & Mac

Having company? This overnight dish can be popped in the oven right before guests arrive.

Serves 6 to 8

2 c. cooked chicken, diced
2 c. elbow macaroni, uncooked
2 c. milk
2 10-3/4 oz. cans cream of mushroom soup
2 onions, diced
8-oz. pkg. pasteurized processed cheese spread, diced

Mix all ingredients together; spoon into an ungreased 13"x9" baking pan. Refrigerate overnight; bake at 350 degrees for one hour.

Dianne Young, South Jordan, UT

Beef & Cheddar Quiche

So tasty topped with sour cream or even salsa!

Makes 8 servings

3 eggs, beaten
1 c. whipping cream
1 c. shredded Cheddar cheese
1 c. ground beef, browned
9-inch pie crust

Mix eggs, cream, cheese and beef together; spread into pie crust. Bake at 450 degrees for 15 minutes; lower oven temperature to 350 degrees and continue baking for 15 minutes.

★ DOUBLE DUTY ★ Have a little pie crust dough left over from your quiche? Bake up a Grandma-style treat...roll out extra pie crust, cut into strips and sprinkle with cinnamon-sugar. Bake at 350 degrees until golden. Dessert is ready!

Cheesy Chicken & Mac

J.J. Presley, Portland, TX

Cheesy Sausage-Potato Casserole

Add some fresh green beans too, if you like.

Serves 6 to 8

3 to 4 potatoes, sliced
2 8-oz. links sausage, sliced into
   2-inch lengths
1 onion, chopped
1/2 c. butter, sliced
1 c. shredded Cheddar cheese

Layer potatoes, sausage and onion in a skillet sprayed with non-stick vegetable spray. Dot with butter; sprinkle with cheese. Bake at 350 degrees for 1-1/2 hours.

Shelia Butts, Creedmoor, NC

Hashbrown Casserole

Such a creamy, filling side dish and it's so easy to make.

Makes 6 servings

10-3/4 oz. can cream of chicken soup
8-oz. container sour cream
1/2 c. margarine, melted and divided
2 c. shredded sharp Cheddar cheese
salt and pepper to taste
30-oz. pkg. frozen shredded
   hashbrowns, thawed
1 c. corn flake cereal, crushed

In a bowl, combine soup, sour cream, half the margarine, shredded cheese, salt and pepper. Pour mixture into a lightly greased 13"x9" baking pan; top with hashbrowns. Mix corn flake cereal and remaining margarine; spread over hashbrowns. Bake, uncovered, at 350 degrees for 30 minutes, or until hot and bubbly.

Cheesy Sausage-Potato Casserole

Alice Ardaugh, Joliet, IL

Zesty Italian Chicken

Not your usual chicken dinner!

Serves 4

4 boneless, skinless chicken breasts
1/2 c. Italian salad dressing, divided
1/2 c. grated Parmesan cheese,
  divided
1 t. Italian seasoning, divided
4 potatoes, quartered

Arrange chicken in a 4-quart slow cooker; sprinkle with half each of salad dressing, Parmesan cheese and Italian seasoning. Add potatoes; top with remaining dressing, cheese and seasoning. Cover and cook on low setting for 8 hours, or on high setting for 4 hours.

Michele Molen, Mendon, UT

Simple Baked Mostaccioli

My Italian grandmother always used this quick & easy recipe when she needed a dish for last-minute company or to send to a sick friend. It will always be a comfort food to me...mangia, mangia!

Serves 5

16-oz. pkg. mostaccioli pasta,
  uncooked
1 lb. ground beef
salt and pepper to taste
16-oz. jar pasta sauce, divided
8-oz. pkg. shredded mozzarella
  cheese, divided

Cook pasta according to package directions; drain. Meanwhile, brown beef in a skillet over medium heat. Drain; season with salt and pepper. Ladle a spoonful of pasta sauce into a greased 2-quart casserole dish; add half of cooked pasta. Layer with all of beef mixture, half of remaining sauce and half of cheese; repeat layers with remaining pasta, sauce and cheese. Bake, uncovered, at 375 degrees for about 20 minutes, until hot and bubbly.

Zesty Italian Chicken

Ellen Forney, Ravenna, OH

Scalloped Chicken

A rotisserie chicken works well in this recipe!

Serves 4 to 6

3 to 4 c. cooked chicken, chopped
10-3/4 oz. can cream of mushroom
    soup
2 c. round buttery crackers, crushed
    and divided
2 T. butter, melted

In a lightly greased 2-quart baking dish, combine chicken, soup and 1/2 cup crackers. Combine remaining crackers with butter and sprinkle over top of chicken mixture. Bake at 350 degrees for 40 minutes.

Carol Wingo, Henderson, TX

Tomato-Beef Noodle Bake

Add a few diced mushrooms when you're browning the beef for extra flavor.

Makes 4 servings

1 lb. ground beef
1 onion, chopped
10-oz. can diced tomatoes with
    green chiles
10-3/4 oz. can cream of mushroom
    soup
8-oz. pkg. fine egg noodles, cooked

Brown beef and onion in a skillet over medium heat; drain. Add remaining ingredients; place in an ungreased 2-quart casserole dish. Bake at 350 degrees for 20 to 25 minutes, until hot and bubbly.

★ MAKE IT CRUNCH ★ A new twist on casserole toppers...try crushed veggie, chicken or cheese-flavored crackers combined with fresh or dried herbs and melted butter. Sprinkle on top before baking for a delicious crunch.

Scalloped Chicken

Jo Ann, Gooseberry Patch

Chicken Lasagna with Roasted Red Pepper Sauce

There's nothing like a hot pan of lasagna on a cold winter's night! The Roasted Red Pepper Sauce is also great over your favorite noodles.

Serves 6 to 8

4 c. cooked chicken, finely chopped
2 8-oz. containers chive & onion cream cheese
10-oz. pkg. frozen chopped spinach, thawed and well drained
1 t. seasoned pepper
3/4 t. garlic salt
9 no-boil lasagna noodles, uncooked
8-oz. pkg. shredded Italian 3-cheese blend

Stir together chicken, cream cheese, spinach and seasonings; set aside. Layer a lightly greased 11"x7" baking pan with 1/3 of Roasted Red Pepper Sauce, 3 noodles, 1/3 of chicken mixture and 1/3 of cheese. Repeat layers twice. Place baking pan on a baking sheet. Bake, covered, at 350 degrees for 50 to 55 minutes or until thoroughly heated. Uncover and bake 15 more minutes.

Roasted Red Pepper Sauce:

12-oz. jar roasted red peppers, drained
16-oz. jar creamy Alfredo sauce
3/4 c. grated Parmesan cheese
1/2 t. red pepper flakes

★ YOUR WAY ★ A fun new spin on a "make your own" bar...let guests assemble their own personal lasagna! Use small aluminum loaf pans and set out an assortment of cooked noodles, cooked and crumbled Italian sausage, steamed veggies, spaghetti sauce, ricotta cheese and shredded mozzarella cheese. Place pans on a baking sheet and bake at 300 degrees for 20 minutes.

Chicken Lasagna with Roasted Red Pepper Sauce

Linda Newkirk, Central Point, OR

Special Spanish Pot Roast

A good friend shared this recipe with me years ago. I've prepared it many times for family and guests.

Serves 4 to 6

8-oz. bottle Catalina salad dressing, divided
3-lb. beef chuck roast
6 to 8 carrots, peeled and diced
6 to 8 potatoes, peeled and diced
Optional: 1 onion, quartered
12-oz. jar green olives with pimentos

Heat 1/4 cup dressing in a roasting pan over medium heat. Add roast to pan; cook and turn until all sides are browned. Add carrots, potatoes and onion, if using, to pan. Pour remaining dressing over all; top with olives and olive juice. Cover and bake at 350 degrees for 2 to 3 hours, to desired doneness.

Bev Bornheimer, Lyons, NY

Penne Sausage Bake

This is also good made with sliced Kielbasa in place of the ground sausage.

Makes 6 to 8 servings

1 lb. hot or mild ground Italian pork sausage
3 cloves garlic, chopped
24-oz. jar marinara sauce with cabernet and herbs
1/2 t. red pepper flakes
1/2 t. salt
1/2 t. pepper
12-oz. pkg. penne pasta, cooked
1 c. shredded mozzarella cheese
Garnish: grated Parmesan cheese, chopped fresh parsley

Cook sausage in a skillet over medium heat until browned; drain. Return sausage to pan. Add garlic and cook until tender, about 2 minutes. Stir in sauce and seasonings. Stir sauce mixture into cooked pasta; pour mixture into a greased 12"x8" baking pan. Top with mozzarella cheese. Bake, covered, at 375 degrees for 25 to 30 minutes, until bubbly and cheese has melted. Remove from oven; sprinkle with Parmesan cheese and parsley.

Special Spanish Pot Roast

Holly Sutton, Middleburgh, NY

Stuffed Pasta Shells

You'll have just enough time to make a crispy salad while this casserole is baking...it's ready in just 30 minutes.

Serves 6 to 8

1-1/2 c. chicken-flavored stuffing
   mix, prepared
2 c. cooked chicken, chopped
1/2 c. peas
1/2 c. mayonnaise
18 jumbo pasta shells, cooked
10-3/4 oz. can cream of chicken
   soup
2/3 c. water

Combine stuffing, chicken, peas and mayonnaise; spoon into cooked pasta shells. Arrange shells in a greased 13"x9" baking pan. Mix soup and water; pour over shells. Cover and bake at 350 degrees for 30 minutes.

Jenny Bishoff, Mountain Lake Park, MD

Meatball-Stuffed Shells

As a working mom with two little girls, I've found this super-easy recipe is great for a quick dinner. The kids can help too!

Serves 6 to 8

12-oz. pkg. jumbo pasta shells,
   uncooked
28-oz. jar pasta sauce, divided
36 frozen Italian meatballs, thawed
2 c. shredded mozzarella cheese
Garnish: grated Parmesan cheese

Cook pasta according to package directions; drain and rinse in cold water. Spread 1/2 cup pasta sauce in a greased 13"x9" baking pan. Tuck a meatball into each shell; arrange shells in pan. Top with remaining sauce; add cheese. Cover; bake at 350 degrees for 35 minutes. Uncover and bake 10 more minutes.

★ HOT TIP ★ For casseroles with already-cooked meat, test for doneness by inserting the tip of a table knife in the center of the casserole. If the knife tip is hot to the touch when pulled out, the casserole should be heated through.

Stuffed Pasta Shells

Tegan Reeves, Auburndale, FL

Crunchy Corn Chip Chicken

Dinner in a jiffy...so quick to whip up!

Makes 6 servings

6 boneless, skinless chicken breasts
10-3/4 oz. can cream of chicken soup
8-oz. pkg. shredded Cheddar cheese,
divided
1-1/4 oz. pkg. taco seasoning mix
2 c. barbecue corn chips, crushed

Arrange chicken in an ungreased 13"x9" baking pan; set aside. Combine soup, one cup cheese and taco seasoning together; spread over chicken. Bake, uncovered, at 450 degrees for 45 minutes; sprinkle with corn chips and remaining cheese. Return to oven; bake until cheese melts, about 5 minutes.

Martha Stephens, Sibley, LA

Spicy Chicken Casserole

A hearty, creamy dinner in one dish...with just four ingredients!

Makes 6 servings

4 to 5 boneless, skinless chicken
breasts
2 10-3/4 oz. cans cream of chicken
soup
2 10-3/4 oz. cans nacho cheese
soup
3 to 4 c. tortilla chips, crushed and
divided

Cover chicken breasts with water in a large saucepan. Simmer over medium-high heat just until cooked through. Drain, saving broth for another use. Cool chicken slightly; shred into bite-size pieces, and set aside. Combine soups in a saucepan. Stir well; cook over medium heat until bubbly. Remove from heat. In a greased 13"x9" baking pan, layer half of chicken, half of soup mixture and half of the crushed chips. Repeat layers. Cover and bake at 350 degrees for 20 minutes or until heated through.

Crunchy Corn Chip Chicken

Kris Coburn, Dansville, NY

Country Chicken Pot Pie

Just like Mom used to make! It's a delicious way to use up leftover chicken and cooked vegetables too.

Serves 4 to 6

2 9-inch pie crusts, divided
1-1/2 c. cooked chicken, diced
2 to 3 c. frozen mixed vegetables, thawed
2 10-3/4 oz. cans cream of chicken soup
1/2 c. milk
1 t. pepper
1 t. dried thyme
1 egg, beaten

Line a 9" pie plate with one crust. Mix together chicken, vegetables, soup, milk, pepper and thyme; spread in crust. Top with remaining crust; cut slits to vent and brush with egg. Bake at 350 degrees for 50 minutes.

Shari Miller, Hobart, IN

Cheeseburger & Fries Casserole

The recipe name says it all...kids will love it!

Makes 6 to 8 servings

2 lbs. ground beef
10-3/4 oz. can golden mushroom soup
10-3/4 oz. can Cheddar cheese soup
20-oz. pkg. frozen crinkle-cut French fries

Brown beef in a large skillet over medium heat; drain. Stir in soups. Spread beef mixture in a greased 13"x9" baking pan; arrange French fries on top. Bake, uncovered, at 350 degrees for 50 to 55 minutes, or until bubbly and fries are golden.

★ SPICED-UP ★ For zesty French fries that are anything but boring, spray frozen fries with non-stick olive oil spray and sprinkle with your favorite spice blend like Italian, Cajun or steak seasoning. Spread on a baking sheet and bake as directed.

Country Chicken Pot Pie

Jennifer Holmes, Philadelphia, PA

Fruity Baked Chicken

Serve over steamed rice with a side of asparagus spears...delicious!

Makes 6 servings

2 T. olive oil
6 boneless, skinless chicken breasts
3 lemons, halved
3 oranges, halved
1 apple, peeled, cored and chopped

Coat the bottom of a 13"x9" baking pan with olive oil; arrange chicken breasts in pan. Squeeze juice from one lemon and one orange over chicken; set aside. Slice remaining lemons and oranges into wedges; cut these in half. Arrange around and on top of chicken breasts; add apple. Cover and bake at 375 degrees for one hour and 45 minutes; uncover for last 30 minutes of baking.

Deborah Clouser, McLean, VA

Creamy Chicken & Biscuits

You can see the smiles on the faces of my entire family when I take this dish out of the oven. It doesn't take long to make and it is so good!

Makes 8 servings

2 c. new redskin potatoes, halved or quartered
2 c. carrots, peeled and sliced
1 onion, diced
3 T. butter
3 T. all-purpose flour
salt and pepper to taste
2 c. milk
1 c. chicken broth
2 cubes chicken bouillon
2 boneless, skinless chicken breasts, cooked and diced
12-oz. tube large refrigerated biscuits, cut into quarters

Cover potatoes, carrots and onion with water in a medium saucepan. Bring to a boil over medium heat; reduce heat and simmer until tender. Drain and set aside. Melt butter in another medium saucepan; stir in flour, salt and pepper, stirring constantly. Gradually add milk, broth and bouillon. Cook until thickened, about 3 to 5 minutes; set aside. Combine chicken and vegetables in a lightly greased 13"x9" baking pan. Pour sauce over top; arrange biscuits over sauce. Bake, uncovered, at 400 degrees for 15 minutes, or until biscuits are golden and sauce is bubbly.

Fruity Baked Chicken

Shannon Reents, Belleville, OH

Taco-Filled Peppers

My family loves stuffed peppers and Mexican food, so I came up with this two-in-one dish for them.

Makes 4 servings

1 lb. ground beef
1-oz. pkg. taco seasoning mix
1 c. salsa
15-1/2 oz. can kidney beans, drained
4 green peppers, tops removed
1 tomato, chopped
1/2 c. shredded Cheddar cheese
Garnish: 1/2 c. sour cream

Brown beef in a skillet over medium heat; drain. Stir in seasoning mix, salsa and beans; bring to a boil. Simmer for 5 minutes. Meanwhile, add peppers to a large saucepan of boiling water. Cook for 3 to 5 minutes; rinse peppers in cold water and drain well. Spoon 1/2 cup beef mixture into each pepper; arrange peppers in an ungreased 9"x9" baking pan. Cover and bake at 350 degrees for 10 to 12 minutes, or until hot and bubbly. Top with tomato and cheese; serve with sour cream.

Kelly Cook, Dunedin, FL

Tamale Pie

Ready-made tamales make this pie oh-so-quick.

Makes 12 servings

2 15-oz. cans beef tamales, divided
15-oz. can chili, divided
9-1/4 oz. pkg. corn chips, divided
1 onion, minced and divided
2 c. shredded Cheddar cheese, divided

Chop one can of tamales; set aside. Spread one cup chili in the bottom of a greased 2-quart casserole dish; layer half the corn chips, half the onion and chopped tamales on top. Sprinkle with half the cheese; repeat layers, ending with whole tamales topped with cheese. Cover and bake at 350 degrees for one hour. Let cool for 10 minutes before serving.

★ DOUBLE DUTY ★ Don't toss that almost-empty pickle jar...make tangy marinated veggies in a jiffy! Just add cut-up cucumbers, green peppers, carrots, cauliflower and other favorite fresh veggies to the remaining pickle juice and refrigerate. Enjoy within a few days.

Taco-Filled Peppers

Scalloped Sweet Potatoes & Apples, Page 146

CHAPTER FOUR

Sweet & Savory Sides

Country Veggie Bake, Page 166

Broccoli-Corn Casserole, Page 142

Shelba Durston, Lodi, CA

Baked Italian Sausage Dressing

This is an adaptation of a friend's mom's recipe. She had brought it here from Italy over 60 years ago, and it was written in Italian, by her grandmother. I do not speak or read Italian, so I watched what they did in the kitchen and made it my way! We actually begin snacking on this as soon as it is assembled, but it does taste better after baking.

Serves 6 to 8

4 c. sourdough bread cubes
1 lb. sweet or spicy Italian ground
   pork sausage
2 c. fennel bulb, cut into 1/2-inch
   cubes
2 c. Swiss chard, ribs removed,
   diced and packed
1 sweet onion, chopped
1 c. celery, diced
2 to 4 cloves garlic, pressed, to taste
2 c. chicken broth

Spread bread cubes on baking sheets to dry ahead of time. Meanwhile, brown sausage in a large skillet over medium heat until about half cooked. Add vegetables and garlic; cook and stir just until tender. Drain; add bread cubes and toss to mix. Add chicken broth to desired consistency; transfer mixture to a greased 3-quart casserole dish. Cover and bake at 350 degrees for 30 minutes, or until heated through.

★ SALAD DAYS ★ There are lots of tasty choices for crisp side salads. Start with greens like romaine lettuce, endive, fennel, Swiss chard and cabbage. Add crunchy apple slices or tender diced pears, a sprinkling of nuts or seeds and perhaps some crumbled feta or blue cheese. Drizzle with a fruity vinaigrette...delicious!

Baked Italian Sausage Dressing

Linda Hendrix, Moundville, MO

Golden Parmesan Roasted Potatoes

Pop into the oven alongside a roast for a homestyle dinner that can't be beat.

Serves 4 to 6

1/4 c. all-purpose flour
1/4 c. grated Parmesan cheese
3/4 t. salt
1/8 t. pepper
6 potatoes, peeled and cut into
    wedges
1/3 c. butter, melted
Garnish: fresh parsley, chopped

Place flour, cheese, salt and pepper in a large plastic zipping bag; mix well. Add potato wedges; shake to coat. Pour butter into a 13"x9" baking pan, tilting to coat; arrange potatoes in pan. Bake, uncovered, at 375 degrees for one hour. Sprinkle with parsley.

Patricia Elmore, Bessemer City, NC

Broccoli & Rice Casserole

I have been cooking this dish for my family for over 40 years, and they still get excited to see this loved dish on the table.

Makes 8 servings

1 c. long-cooking rice, uncooked
1 onion, chopped
3 stalks celery, chopped
1 c. butter, divided
10-oz. pkg. frozen chopped broccoli,
    thawed and drained
16-oz. jar pasteurized process cheese
    sauce
10-3/4 oz. can cream of mushroom
    soup
1 c. sour cream
1 sleeve round buttery crackers,
    crushed

Cook rice according to package directions; set aside. Sauté onion and celery for 3 minutes in 1/2 cup butter. Mix all ingredients except remaining butter and crackers in a greased 2-quart casserole dish; top with crackers. Melt remaining butter and drizzle over crackers. Bake, uncovered, at 350 degrees for 35 minutes, or until heated through.

Golden Parmesan Roasted Potatoes

Marlene Campbell, Millinocket, ME

Aunt Fran's Cheddar Potatoes

This recipe is shared in memory of my mom, who passed away in 2015. Such a wonderful cook herself, Mom always loved her sister Fran's potato casserole and enjoyed serving it as a special treat for holiday meals.

Serves 8 to 10

6 potatoes, peeled and cubed
8-oz. pkg. shredded Cheddar cheese
1/4 c. butter
1-1/2 c. sour cream
1/3 c. onion, minced
1/4 t. pepper

In a large saucepan, cover potatoes with water. Bring to a boil over high heat. Cook until potatoes are fork-tender; drain. In another saucepan over very low heat, melt together cheese and butter, stirring often. Stir in sour cream, onion and pepper; fold in potatoes. Spoon mixture into a 3-quart casserole dish sprayed with non-stick vegetable spray. Bake, uncovered, at 350 degrees for 30 to 35 minutes, until bubbly and golden.

Pat Wissler, Harrisburg, PA

Cheesy Baked Tortellini

When I make this hearty dish, I usually double the recipe and freeze some for later...very convenient!

Serves 4 to 6

10-oz. pkg. refrigerated cheese tortellini
2 c. marinara sauce
1/3 c. mascarpone cheese or softened cream cheese
1/4 c. fresh Italian parsley, chopped
2 t. fresh thyme, chopped
5 slices smoked mozzarella cheese
1/4 c. shredded Parmesan cheese

Prepare tortellini according to package directions; drain and set aside. Meanwhile, in a bowl, combine marinara sauce, mascarpone or cream cheese, parsley and thyme. Fold in tortellini. Transfer to a greased 9"x9" baking pan. Top with mozzarella and Parmesan cheeses. Bake, covered, at 350 degrees for about 30 minutes, or until cheese is melted and sauce is bubbly.

Aunt Fran's Cheddar Potatoes

Regina Wickline, Pebble Beach, CA

Harvest Casserole

This casserole is packed full of wonderful vegetables grown in your own backyard or from the nearest farmers' market.

Makes 6 servings

1/2 c. long-cooking rice, uncooked
4 redskin potatoes, cut into thin
   wedges
1/4 c. butter, sliced and divided
1 T. fresh sage, chopped
3 red peppers, chopped
1 onion, sliced
2 zucchini, thinly sliced
1 c. shredded Cheddar cheese

Cook rice according to package directions; set aside. Place potatoes in a greased 2-1/2 quart casserole dish. Dot with half the butter; layer half the sage, peppers, onion, zucchini and rice. Layer ingredients again; cover with aluminum foil. Bake at 350 degrees for one hour, or until potatoes are tender. Remove foil; sprinkle cheese over top and return to oven until cheese is melted.

Shirley Howie, Foxboro, MA

Cheesy Lentils & Rice Casserole

This is such a delicious low-fat casserole. My husband requests it all the time!

Serves 4 to 6

3/4 c. dried lentils, uncooked
1/2 c. long-cooking rice, uncooked
3 c. chicken broth
2 T. dried, minced onion
1/2 t. dried basil
1/4 t. dried oregano
1/4 t. dried thyme
1/4 t. garlic powder
3/4 c. shredded Cheddar cheese

Blend all ingredients except cheese in a 2-quart casserole dish. Bake, covered, at 300 degrees for one hour and 15 minutes. Uncover and top with cheese; bake for 15 minutes, or until cheese is melted.

★ VARIETY FOR FUN ★ Dried lentils come in green, black, yellow and the familiar brown color. Each type cooks a little differently, and has their own unique flavor. Try them all or mix & match!

Harvest Casserole

Melanie Springer, Canton, OH

Broccoli-Corn Casserole

My mom used to make this tasty side dish for holiday dinners. It is a favorite of all who try it. I make it, my kids make it and I have shared this recipe with so many people.

Makes 4 servings

10-oz. pkg. frozen chopped broccoli,
   thawed and squeezed dry
16-oz. can creamed corn
1 egg, beaten
1 T. minced dried onion
salt and pepper to taste
3 T. butter, melted and divided
18 saltine crackers, coarsely crushed
   and divided

In a bowl, combine broccoli, creamed corn, egg, onion, seasonings, 2 tablespoons melted butter and 2/3 of cracker crumbs. Mix well; transfer to a greased one-quart casserole dish. In a small bowl; toss together remaining cracker crumbs and butter; sprinkle over casserole. Bake, uncovered, at 350 degrees for about 40 minutes, until hot and bubbly. For a double or triple recipe, use a 13"x9" baking pan; bake about 50 minutes. May be made ahead and reheated.

★ TASTY TIP ★ Homemade savory crackers make a tasty topping for casseroles. Spread saltines with softened butter, then sprinkle with garlic salt, paprika or another favorite seasoning. Pop into a 350-degree oven just until golden, 3 to 6 minutes.

Broccoli-Corn Casserole

Colleen McAleavey, Plum, PA

Cheesy Vegetable Casserole

We like to vary this casserole by choosing different blends of frozen vegetables.

Serves 6 to 8

2 16-oz. pkgs. frozen stir-fry
   blend vegetables, thawed and
   drained
16-oz. pkg. pasteurized process
   cheese spread
1/4 c. milk
1/2 c. butter
1 sleeve round buttery crackers,
   crushed

Place vegetables in a lightly greased 13"x9" baking pan; set aside. Melt cheese in a saucepan over low heat; add milk. Stir until smooth; pour over vegetables. Melt butter and stir in cracker crumbs; sprinkle over vegetables. Bake, uncovered, at 350 degrees for 20 to 25 minutes, until heated through.

Dani Simmers, Kendallville, IN

Zucchini-Corn Casserole

This recipe came from my friend's great-aunt...it tastes wonderful and is pretty easy to fix, too!

Serves 6 to 8

3 lbs. zucchini, cubed
2 c. corn
1 onion, chopped
1 green pepper, chopped
2 T. butter
salt and pepper to taste
4 eggs, lightly beaten
1 c. shredded Cheddar cheese
paprika to taste

In a saucepan, cook zucchini in boiling water for 2 to 3 minutes; drain and set aside. In a skillet over medium heat, sauté corn, onion and green pepper in butter until crisp-tender. Remove from heat and add zucchini to corn mixture; season with salt and pepper and let cool slightly. Stir in eggs and transfer to a greased 13"x9" baking pan. Top with cheese and paprika. Bake, uncovered, at 350 degrees for 40 minutes, or until lightly golden and bubbly.

Cheesy Vegetable Casserole

Michelle Powell, Valley, AL

Scalloped Sweet Potatoes & Apples

Top with a handful of chopped pecans for extra crunch, if you like. Great with ham!

Makes 6 servings

2 sweet potatoes, boiled, peeled and sliced
2 tart apples, peeled, cored and sliced
1/2 c. brown sugar, packed
1/4 c. butter, sliced
1 t. salt

Layer half the potatoes in a buttered 13"x9" baking pan. Layer half the apple slices. Sprinkle with half the sugar; dot with half the butter. Repeat with remaining ingredients. Bake, uncovered, at 350 degrees for one hour.

Regina Ferrigno, Delaware, OH

Spiced Baked Fruit

Guests "ooh" and "ahh" when they discover the rows of fruit under the pineapple...so pretty!

Serves 6 to 8

16-oz. can apricot halves, drained
16-oz. can pear halves, drained
29-oz. can peach halves, drained
8-oz. can pineapple slices, drained and 1/2 c. juice reserved
1/3 c. brown sugar, packed
1 T. butter
1/2 t. cinnamon
1/4 t. ground cloves

In a greased 13"x9" baking pan, starting at the short end, arrange rows of fruit in the following order: half the apricots, half the pears and half the peaches. Repeat rows. Arrange pineapple over fruit. In a saucepan over medium heat, combine reserved pineapple juice and remaining ingredients. Cook and stir until sugar is dissolved and butter is melted. Pour over fruit. Bake, uncovered, at 350 degrees for 20 to 25 minutes, until heated through.

Scalloped Sweet Potatoes & Apples

Patricia Tilley, Sabine, WV

Oven-Fried Bacon Potatoes

Sprinkle with a little shredded Cheddar cheese if you like...tasty!

Serves 6 to 8

3 T. butter, melted
1-1/2 lb. redskin potatoes, cut into
   1/4-inch slices
1/4 t. salt
1/4 t. pepper
6 slices bacon
Garnish: fresh thyme leaves

Coat a cast-iron skillet with melted butter. Layer potatoes in skillet; season each layer with salt and pepper. Arrange uncooked bacon slices on top. Bake, uncovered, at 425 degrees for 40 minutes, or until bacon is crisp and potatoes are tender. Garnish with thyme leaves.

Kelly Patrick, Ashburn, VA

Summer Squash Pie

My mother and I have used this recipe every summer when summer squash is abundant. It's a very simple, one-bowl recipe that takes literally five minutes to toss together...it's never failed us! Feel free to try different cheeses or add your favorite chopped veggies.

Serves 6 to 8

3 c. yellow squash, peeled and diced
1/2 c. onion, chopped
4 eggs, beaten
1/3 c. canola oil
1 c. biscuit baking mix
1/2 c. shredded mozzarella cheese
salt and pepper to taste

Mix all ingredients in a bowl. Pat into a 9" pie plate lightly coated with non-stick vegetable spray. Bake at 350 degrees for 50 minutes to one hour, until set. Let stand for 10 minutes; slice into wedges. Serve warm or cold.

★ DOUBLE DUTY ★ Fry a couple of extra bacon slices when preparing Oven-Fried Bacon Potatoes. Tomorrow's lunch is ready when you add juicy tomato slices and lettuce for a fresh BLT sandwich!

Oven-Fried Bacon Potatoes

Billie Schettino, Kansas City, KS

Mom's Macaroni & Cheese

Mom made this recipe for meatless Fridays. I always looked forward to it, even though I didn't like the spinach she served with it. Before I could eat my mac & cheese I had to eat at least one spoonful of spinach, which I did, and quickly washed it down with a big gulp of milk. It was worth it!

Serves 2 to 4

1 c. elbow macaroni, uncooked
salt and pepper to taste
2 c. shredded American-Cheddar
  Jack cheese blend, divided
1 egg
1/2 c. skim milk
1/2 c. cottage cheese
2 to 3 T. butter, diced

Cook macaroni according to package directions; drain. Place half of macaroni into a 2-quart casserole dish coated with butter-flavored non-stick vegetable spray. Sprinkle macaroni with salt, pepper and one cup shredded cheese. Repeat layering. In a food processor, process egg, milk and cottage cheese until smooth. Pour mixture over top; dot with butter. Bake, uncovered, at 350 degrees for 30 to 45 minutes, until heated throughand set. Cool slightly before serving.

★ HEALTHY BLEND ★ It's easy to get more veggies into your family's meals. Keep frozen vegetable blends on hand to toss into scrambled eggs, chicken noodle soup or mac & cheese for lunch with a veggie punch!

Mom's Macaroni & Cheese

Donna Maltman, Toledo, OH

Family-Favorite Corn Soufflé

An absolute must-have for Thanksgiving dinner.

Serves 8 to 10

15-oz. can corn, drained
8-1/2 oz. pkg. cornbread mix
14-3/4 oz. can creamed corn
1 c. sour cream
1/4 c. butter, melted
8-oz. pkg. shredded Cheddar cheese

Combine all ingredients except cheese. Pour into a lightly greased 13"x9" baking pan or into 8 lightly greased ramekins. Cover with aluminum foil. Bake at 350 degrees for 30 minutes. Uncover; top with cheese. Return to oven and continue baking until cheese is bubbly and golden, about 15 minutes.

Paula Smith, Ottawa, IL

Quick & Easy Parmesan Asparagus

This dish is tasty hot or cold!

Serves 8 to 10

4 lbs. asparagus, trimmed
1/4 c. butter, melted
2 c. shredded Parmesan cheese
1 t. salt
1/2 t. pepper

In a large skillet, add asparagus and one inch of water. Bring to a boil. Reduce heat; cover and simmer for 5 to 7 minutes, until crisp-tender. Drain and arrange asparagus in a greased 13"x9" baking pan. Drizzle with butter; sprinkle with Parmesan cheese, salt and pepper. Bake, uncovered, at 350 degrees for 10 to 15 minutes, until cheese is melted.

★ ADD VEGGIES ★ **Add some fresh broccoli or asparagus to a favorite pasta recipe...simply drop chopped veggies into the pasta pot about halfway through the cooking time. Pasta and veggies will be tender at about the same time.**

Family-Favorite Corn Soufflé

Debbie Wilson, Weatherford, TX

Green Chile Rice

Sprinkle with diced jalapeño peppers for an extra kick!

Serves 6

4 c. cooked rice
8-oz. pkg. shredded mozzarella cheese
2 c. sour cream
4-oz. can diced green chiles, drained

Combine all ingredients in an ungreased 2-quart casserole dish. Mix well. Bake, uncovered, at 400 degrees until bubbly, about 20 minutes.

Lynn Filipowicz, Wilmington, NC

Pineapple Casserole

I have been making this dish for years... it's good hot or cold.

Makes 8 servings

20-oz. can crushed pineapple
20-oz. can pineapple chunks, drained
2 c. shredded sharp Cheddar cheese
1/4 c. sugar
6 T. all-purpose flour
1 sleeve round buttery crackers, crushed
1/2 c. butter, melted
Optional: pineapple rings, maraschino cherries

Mix together pineapple, cheese, sugar and flour in a greased 13"x9" baking pan. Top with crackers; drizzle butter over top. Bake, uncovered, at 350 degrees for about 30 minutes, or until heated through and bubbly. Garnish with pineapple rings and cherries, if desired.

Green Chile Rice

Tina Goodpasture, Meadowview, VA

Parmesan Scalloped Potatoes

Whether you eat them hot, cold or warm...these are some great scalloped potatoes!

Makes 8 servings

2 lbs. Yukon Gold potatoes, thinly
   sliced
3 c. whipping cream
1/4 c. fresh parsley, chopped
2 cloves garlic, chopped
1-1/2 t. salt
1/4 t. pepper
1/3 c. grated Parmesan cheese

Layer potatoes in a lightly greased 3-quart casserole dish. In a bowl, stir together remaining ingredients except cheese; pour over potatoes. Bake, uncovered, at 400 degrees for 30 minutes, stirring gently every 10 minutes. Sprinkle with cheese; bake again for about 15 minutes, or until bubbly and golden. Let stand 10 minutes before serving.

Valerie Hendrickson, Cedar Springs, MI

Mom's Cheesy Hashbrowns

My mother used to make this scrumptious dish the old-fashioned way, starting with hand-shredded boiled potatoes. This version is simplified using frozen shredded potatoes, yet is still full of hearty homestyle flavor!

Serves 6 to 8

1/4 c. butter
1 sweet onion, chopped
2 c. shredded Cheddar cheese
1 c. sour cream
30-oz. pkg. frozen country-style
   shredded hashbrowns, thawed

Melt butter in a medium saucepan over medium heat. Add onion and cook until translucent, about 5 minutes. Mix in cheese and continue stirring until melted. Remove from heat; stir in sour cream. Gently fold mixture into hashbrowns. Spoon into a greased 2-quart casserole dish. Bake, uncovered, at 350 degrees for 60 to 75 minutes, until heated through and top is golden.

Parmesan Scalloped Potatoes

Jennifer Niemi, Nova Scotia, Canada

Rosemary Peppers & Fusilli

This colorful, flavorful meatless meal is ready to serve in a jiffy. If you can't find fusilli pasta, try medium shells, rotini or even wagon wheels.

Makes 4 servings

2 to 4 T. olive oil
2 red onions, thinly sliced and
   separated into rings
3 red, orange and/or yellow peppers,
   very thinly sliced
5 to 6 cloves garlic, very thinly
   sliced
3 t. dried rosemary
salt and pepper to taste
12-oz. pkg. fusilli pasta, cooked
Optional: shredded mozzarella
   cheese

Add oil to a large skillet over medium heat. Add onions to skillet; cover and cook over medium heat for 10 minutes. Stir in remaining ingredients except pasta and cheese; reduce heat. Cook, covered, stirring occasionally, for an additional 20 minutes. Serve vegetable mixture over pasta, topped with cheese if desired.

Joann Sklarsky, Johnstown, PA

Sweet Potato-Apple Bake

A deliciously sweet side dish that goes great with chicken, pork or beef.

Makes 6 to 8 servings

29-oz. can sweet potatoes
21-oz. can apple pie filling
16-oz. can whole-berry cranberry
   sauce

Carefully fold ingredients together; spread into a buttered 2-quart casserole dish. Bake at 350 degrees until heated through, about 30 to 45 minutes.

★ SAVVY SWAP ★ Pasta shapes like bowties, seashells and corkscrew-shaped cavatappi all work well in casseroles...why not give a favorite casserole a whole new look?

Rosemary Peppers & Fusilli

Vickie, Gooseberry Patch

Wild Mushroom & Thyme Spoon Bread

You'll love this dressed-up southern favorite.

Makes 8 servings

2 T. oil, divided
1 onion, chopped
2 cloves garlic, minced
1 T. fresh thyme, minced
4-oz. pkg. cremini mushrooms, sliced
4-oz. pkg. shiitake mushrooms, sliced
2 c. chicken broth
1 t. seasoned salt
1 c. cornmeal
1 c. milk
4 eggs, separated
Optional: fresh thyme sprigs

Heat one tablespoon oil in a large skillet over medium-high heat. Add onion, garlic and thyme; sauté until softened, 3 to 5 minutes. Set aside.

Reduce heat to low; add remaining oil and mushrooms to skillet. Cover and cook until liquid evaporates, about 8 minutes, stirring occasionally. Stir in onion mixture, reserving 1/2 cup mixture for topping. In a saucepan over high heat, bring broth and salt to a boil. Gradually add cornmeal, whisking well; cook and stir for one minute. Remove from heat; stir in mushroom mixture, milk and egg yolks. Beat egg whites until stiff with an electric mixer on high speed; gently fold into cornmeal mixture. Pour into a 2-quart casserole dish that has been sprayed with non-stick vegetable spray. Bake at 400 degrees for 35 to 40 minutes, until puffy and set. Warm reserved mushroom mixture; spoon over top. Garnish with fresh thyme sprigs, if desired.

★ TOP IT OFF ★ Did you buy a bunch of fresh herbs for a recipe that calls for just a couple of tablespoons? Chop the extra herbs and add to a tossed salad! Fresh dill, parsley, thyme, chives and basil all add "zing" to salads.

Wild Mushroom & Thyme Spoon Bread

Eva Rae Walter, Paola, KS

Corn Surprise

A winter warm-up recipe that's easy to double, making it perfect for potlucks.

Serves 6 to 8

15-1/4 oz. can corn
8-oz. pkg. small pasta shells, uncooked
16-oz. can cream-style corn
8-oz. pkg. shredded Mexican-blend cheese

Combine undrained corn and remaining ingredients in a bowl. Transfer to a greased 13"x9" baking pan. Bake, covered, at 350 degrees for 45 minutes, or until pasta is tender. As it bakes, stir casserole several times; uncover for the last 10 minutes of cooking..

Nola Coons, Gooseberry Patch

Hawaiian Baked Beans

Pineapple, baked beans and brown sugar...yum! If you're not feeding a crowd, it's simple to halve this recipe and bake it in an 8"x8" pan.

Serves 8 to 12

1-3/4 c. pineapple juice
1 c. catsup
1/2 c. mustard
1-1/2 c. dark brown sugar, packed
15-oz. can pineapple chunks, drained
4 15-1/2 oz. cans navy beans & bacon, drained and rinsed

In a bowl, whisk together pineapple juice, catsup and mustard. Add brown sugar and mix well; stir in pineapple chunks. Add beans; mix well. Spoon into a greased 13"x9" baking pan. Bake, uncovered, at 350 degrees for 90 minutes, or until hot and bubbly.

Corn Surprise

Marcia Emig, Goodland, KS

Golden Homestyle Rice

This tasty rice offers a nice change of pace from potatoes.

Serves 4

1 c. long-cooking rice, uncooked
1 T. butter
1/2 c. green onions, chopped
1/2 lb. sliced mushrooms
1-1/2 c. chicken broth
1/2 c. dry sherry or chicken broth
1 t. salt
1 t. pepper
Garnish: chopped green onions

Pour uncooked rice into a greased 11"x7" baking pan; set aside. Melt butter in a saucepan over medium heat; add green onions and sauté until soft. Add mushrooms and sauté until soft. Add chicken broth, sherry or broth, salt and pepper; bring to a boil. Remove from heat and pour over rice in baking pan. Cover and bake at 375 degrees for 25 to 30 minutes. Garnish with additional green onions.

Wendy Reaume, Ontario, Canada

Cheesy Chile Rice

When I was growing up, my mom made this simple rice dish whenever we had Mexican food for dinner. It's yummy with burritos and tortilla chips.

Makes 6 servings

2 c. water
2 c. instant rice, uncooked
16-oz. container sour cream
4-oz. can diced green chiles
3 c. shredded Cheddar cheese, divided

In a saucepan over medium-high heat, bring water to a boil. Stir in rice; remove from heat. Cover and let stand 5 minutes, until water is absorbed. In a large bowl, mix together rice, sour cream, chiles and 2 cups cheese. Spread in a greased 2-quart casserole dish; top with remaining cheese. Bake, uncovered, at 400 degrees for 30 minutes, or until cheese is melted and top is lightly golden.

Golden Homestyle Rice

Pat Griedl, Appleton, WI

Country Veggie Bake

One of our favorite meatless meals!

Makes 6 servings

1 to 2 T. olive oil
2 carrots, peeled, halved lengthwise
   and sliced
2 onions, chopped
1 to 2 cloves garlic, chopped
1 c. mushrooms, quartered
15-oz. can black beans, drained and
   rinsed
14-oz. can vegetable or chicken
   broth
1 c. frozen corn
1/2 c. pearled barley, uncooked
1/4 c. bulghur wheat, uncooked

1/3 c. fresh parsley, snipped
dried thyme to taste
1/2 to 1 c. shredded Cheddar cheese

Heat oil in a large skillet over medium heat. Sauté carrots and onions until carrots are tender. Stir in garlic and mushrooms; sauté 3 minutes. Combine mixture with remaining ingredients except cheese. Spoon into a greased 2-quart casserole dish. Bake, covered, at 350 degrees for one hour, stirring once halfway through baking time. Top with cheese. Cover and let stand 5 minutes, or until cheese melts.

★ HANDY TIP ★ Make a kettle of soup using pearled barley and refrigerate it overnight...the barley will absorb the broth and swell. The next day, just thin it with a little extra broth or water while reheating the soup. Extra soup servings...almost free!

Country Veggie Bake

Susan Fountain, Stanton, MI

Grandma Dumeney's Baked Beans

My Grandma Dumeney brought her sweet baked beans to every family reunion...everyone really looked forward to them! Grandma was eighty-four when she shared this simple recipe with me, and I'm so glad she did!

Makes 8 servings

3 28-oz. cans pork & beans
1 lb. bacon, crisply cooked and
    crumbled
1 c. brown sugar, packed
1 c. catsup
1 onion, diced

Combine all ingredients in a large bowl and mix well. Transfer to a lightly greased 4-quart casserole dish with a lid. Bake, covered, at 400 degrees for one hour. Reduce temperature to 350 degrees; uncover dish and bake for an additional hour.

Robyn Burton, Thornville, OH

Green Bean Delight

An old standby dressed up with shredded cheese and nuts.

Serves 8 to 10

4 16-oz. cans green beans, drained
1-oz. pkg. ranch salad dressing mix
2 10-3/4 oz. cans cream of
    mushroom soup
1/4 c. milk
8-oz. pkg. shredded Colby Jack
    cheese
1 c. sliced almonds or cashews
2.8-oz. can French fried onions

Spread green beans in a lightly greased 13"x9" baking pan; set aside. Combine salad dressing mix, soup and milk in a bowl; drizzle over beans. Sprinkle with cheese, nuts and onions. Bake, uncovered, at 350 degrees for 25 minutes.

★ NUTTY MIX ★ Chop together a mix of pecans, walnuts, peanuts, almonds or cashews and use the combination in your recipes. You can freeze the mix and use as needed.

Grandma Dumeney's Baked Beans

Mary Ellen Dawson, Boise, ID

Sweet Corn & Rice Casserole

Roll up leftovers in a flour tortilla for a hearty snack.

Serves 10 to 12

2 T. butter
1 green pepper, chopped
1 onion, chopped
15-1/2 oz. can creamed corn
11-oz. can sweet corn & diced
   peppers, drained
11-oz. can corn, drained
6 c. cooked rice
10-oz. can diced tomatoes with
   green chiles, drained
8-oz. pkg. mild Mexican pasteurized
   process cheese spread, cubed
1/2 t. salt
1/4 t. pepper
1/2 c. shredded Cheddar cheese

Melt butter in a large skillet over medium heat. Add green pepper and onion; sauté 5 minutes, or until tender. Stir in remaining ingredients except shredded cheese; spoon into a lightly greased 13"x9" baking pan. Bake, uncovered, at 350 degrees for 25 to 30 minutes, until heated through. Top with shredded cheese; bake an additional 5 minutes, or until cheese melts.

★ FREEZE IT ★ One way to enjoy fresh corn year 'round for casseroles and side dishes is to freeze it...and it's so simple! Husk ears and stack them in a large pot, cover with water, bring to a boil and cook for 5 minutes. Remove ears and chill in ice water until they're cool enough to handle. Cut the kernels from the cobs and store in freezer bags.

Sweet Corn & Rice Casserole

Lisa Ashton, Aston, PA

White Cheddar-Cauliflower Casserole

Lots of cheese and bacon will have the kids eating their cauliflower in this terrific casserole.

Makes 6 servings

1 head cauliflower, cooked and
   mashed
8-oz. pkg. shredded white Cheddar
   cheese, divided
1/2 lb. bacon, crisply cooked,
   crumbled and divided
1/2 c. cream cheese, softened
2 T. sour cream
salt and pepper to taste

Combine cauliflower, half the Cheddar cheese and 3/4 of the bacon in a bowl. Add cream cheese and sour cream; mix well. Spread mixture in a greased 8"x8" baking pan; top with remaining Cheddar cheese and bacon. Sprinkle with salt and pepper. Bake, uncovered, at 350 degrees for 20 to 25 minutes, until bubbly and golden around edges.

Gloria Robertson, Midland, TX

Spinach Soufflé

Add a few chopped mushrooms if you like!

Makes 6 servings

10-oz. pkg. frozen, chopped
   spinach, thawed
3 T. all-purpose flour
3 eggs, beaten
1/2 t. salt
12-oz. container cottage cheese
1 c. shredded Cheddar cheese
1/4 c. butter, melted

In a large mixing bowl, combine spinach with flour; add eggs, salt, cottage cheese, Cheddar cheese and butter. Place in a greased 13"x9" baking pan. Bake, covered, at 375 degrees for 45 minutes. Uncover and bake an additional 15 minutes.

★ HOT SIDE ★ Bake a panful of roasted vegetables alongside a casserole. Slice, cube or trim zucchini, cauliflower, sweet peppers, mushrooms, asparagus and other veggies of your choice. Toss with olive oil and spread on a jelly-roll pan. Bake at 350 degrees for 30 to 35 minutes, stirring occasionally, until tender.

White Cheddar-Cauliflower Casserole

Stephanie Norton, Saginaw, TX

Company Green Beans

A simple way to jazz up green beans.

Makes 4 servings

3 slices bacon
1/4 c. red onion, finely grated
2 t. garlic, minced
2 14-1/2 oz. cans French-style
   green beans, drained
1 tomato, chopped
salt and pepper to taste
1/2 c. shredded sharp Cheddar
   cheese

Cook bacon in a cast-iron skillet over medium-high heat until crisp. Remove bacon to paper towels, reserving drippings in skillet. Sauté onion and garlic in reserved drippings until slightly softened. Remove from heat; stir in green beans, tomato and seasonings. Sprinkle with cheese. Cover the skillet and transfer to oven. Bake at 400 degrees for 15 minutes. Uncover; reduce heat to 350 degrees. Bake an additional 15 minutes, until hot and bubbly.

Jo Ann, Gooseberry Patch

Mexican Veggie Bake

Layers of tasty sautéed fresh vegetables and melted cheese... perfect for a meatless Monday.

Makes 6 servings

1/2 c. green pepper, finely chopped
1/2 c. carrot, peeled and finely
   chopped
1/2 c. celery, finely chopped
1/2 c. onion, finely chopped
2 c. cooked rice
16-oz. can refried beans
15-oz. can black beans, drained
   and rinsed
1 c. salsa
12-oz. pkg. shredded Cheddar
   cheese, divided

Sauté vegetables in a lightly greased skillet over medium heat until tender, about 5 minutes. Transfer vegetables to a large bowl; add remaining ingredients except cheese. Layer half of mixture in a lightly greased 13"x9" baking pan; sprinkle with half of cheese. Repeat layering, ending with cheese. Bake, uncovered, at 350 degrees until heated through, about 15 to 20 minutes.

Company Green Beans

SWEET & SAVORY SIDES

Joan White, Malvern, PA

Simple Scalloped Tomatoes

This tangy-sweet dish makes a delicious dinner. Serve with cheese bread for a complete meal.

Serves 4 to 6

1 onion, chopped
1/4 c. butter
28-oz. can diced tomatoes
5 slices bread, lightly toasted and cubed
1/4 c. brown sugar, packed
1/2 t. salt
1/4 t. pepper

Cook onion in butter until just tender, but not browned. Combine onion mixture with tomatoes and their juice in a bowl; add remaining ingredients, and mix well. Pour into a greased 8"x8" baking pan. Bake, uncovered, at 350 degrees for 45 minutes..

Patricia Rozzelle, Mineral Bluff, GA

Sugared Sweet Potatoes

A perfect side for pork chops!

Serves 10 to 12

1-1/2 c. brown sugar, packed
1/4 c. margarine
3/4 t. salt
1 t. vanilla extract
1 c. cola
9 sweet potatoes, boiled and sliced

In a medium saucepan, cook brown sugar, margarine, salt, vanilla and cola; bring to a boil for 5 minutes. Arrange potatoes in an ungreased 13"x9" baking pan. Pour brown sugar mixture over potatoes. Bake, uncovered, at 350 degrees for 25 to 30 minutes until edges are crisp.

★ HANDY TIP ★ **Turn Simple Scalloped Tomatoes into a hearty main dish...simply add cubes of baked ham along with the tomatoes. Delicious!**

CHAPTER FIVE

Slow-Cooker Sides & Suppers

Chicken Parmigiana, Page 196

Caribbean Chicken & Veggies, Page 186

Erin Hibshman, Lebanon, PA

No-Fuss Chicken Dinner

Perfect for those busy days when everyone has someplace else to be... it tastes as if you spent hours over the stove!

Serves 4 to 6

4 to 6 chicken breasts
4 baking potatoes, quartered
1/2 lb. baby carrots
1 onion, chopped
10-3/4 oz. can cream of chicken soup
1/4 t. garlic powder
2 to 4 T. water

Place chicken in a large slow cooker; arrange vegetables around chicken. In a bowl, stir together soup, garlic powder and enough water to make it pourable. Spoon soup mixture over chicken and vegetables. Cover and cook on low setting for 7 to 8 hours, stirring once after 4 hours, if possible.

Shari Upchurch, Dearing, GA

Provincial Chicken

I've tweaked this recipe over the years...now it's just the way my family likes it!

Makes 6 servings

4 boneless, skinless chicken breasts
2 15-oz. cans diced tomatoes
2 zucchini, diced
10-3/4 oz. can cream of chicken soup
2 T. balsamic vinegar
1 T. dried, minced onion
2 T. dried parsley
1 t. dried basil
1 c. shredded Cheddar cheese
1/2 c. sour cream
cooked bowtie pasta

In a slow cooker, combine chicken, tomatoes with juice, zucchini, soup, vinegar, onion and herbs. Cover and cook on low setting for 6 to 8 hours. Remove chicken; cut into bite-size pieces and return to slow cooker. Stir in cheese and sour cream; cover and cook for an additional 15 minutes. To serve, spoon over cooked pasta.

No-Fuss Chicken Dinner

Jenessa Yauch, Munhall, PA

Ropa Vieja

This is an old Cuban recipe which literally translates to "old clothes." It is very flavorful.

Makes 8 servings

1 T. olive oil
2-lb. beef flank steak or London broil
8-oz. can tomato sauce
6-oz. can tomato paste
1 c. beef broth
1/2 c. yellow onion, diced
1 green pepper, sliced into strips
1 T. vinegar
2 cloves garlic, minced
1 t. ground cumin
1 t. dried cilantro
4 c. cooked brown rice

Heat oil in a skillet over medium heat; brown beef on both sides. Drain; transfer to a slow cooker. Add remaining ingredients except rice; stir. Cover and cook on low setting for 8 hours, or on high setting for 4 hours, until beef is tender. Shred beef in slow cooker; stir well and serve over cooked rice.

Sonya Collett, Sioux City, IA

Zesty Picante Chicken

Spice up suppertime with yummy southwestern-style chicken breasts...made in the slow cooker! Cheese and picante sauce combine for a zesty and flavorful tang and the black beans add great texture.

Makes 4 servings

4 boneless, skinless chicken breasts, browned
16-oz. jar picante sauce
15-1/2 oz. can black beans, drained and rinsed
4 slices Cheddar cheese
2-1/4 c. cooked rice
Optional: sliced green onions

Place chicken in a 5-quart slow cooker; add picante sauce. Spread black beans over the top. Cover and cook on high setting for 3 hours or until juices run clear when chicken is pierced with a fork. Top with cheese slices; cover and cook until melted. Spoon over rice to serve. Garnish with green onions, if desired.

Ropa Vieja

Teresa Eller, Kansas City, KS

Busy-Day Spinach Lasagna

Great for having ready in advance, working late and company coming. Dinner will be ready when you get home from work...just add some garlic toast and a crisp salad.

Serves 6 to 8

2 lbs. extra-lean ground beef
2 T. Italian seasoning, divided
2 14-1/2 oz. cans diced tomatoes, divided
2 8-oz. cans tomato sauce, divided
6 c. fresh spinach, torn and divided
3 c. shredded Swiss or mozzarella cheese, divided
12-oz. pkg. lasagna noodles, uncooked and broken up

Break up uncooked beef and place in a slow cooker sprayed with non-stick vegetable spray. Sprinkle beef with one tablespoon Italian seasoning. Add one can tomatoes with juice and one can tomato sauce; stir gently to combine. Add half of spinach; press down gently. Add one cup cheese and half of uncooked noodles. Repeat layers, ending with cheese on top. Cover and cook on low setting for 8 hours.

★ FRESH BAKED ★ While dinner cooks, why not pop some Parmesan bread in the oven? Blend 1/4 cup butter, 2 tablespoons grated Parmesan cheese, 2 teaspoons minced garlic and 1/4 teaspoon Italian seasoning. Spread it over a halved loaf of French bread and broil until golden.

Busy-Day Spinach Lasagna

Amy Bradsher, Roxboro, NC

Caribbean Chicken & Veggies

I love to serve meals made from scratch, but they can be pretty time-consuming. This recipe is super-simple and cooks on its own, requiring little attention from me. Best of all, my kids love it!

Serves 4 to 6

1 lb. boneless, skinless chicken
   tenders
1 c. canned diced pineapple with
   juice
1 onion, coarsely chopped
1 green pepper, coarsely chopped
3/4 c. Caribbean-style marinade
2 c. canned black beans, drained
1 lb. broccoli, cut into bite-size
   flowerets
cooked rice

Combine chicken, pineapple with juice, onion, green pepper and marinade in a slow cooker. Cover and cook on low setting for 4 to 5 hours, until chicken is nearly cooked. Add black beans and broccoli. Cover and cook for another hour, or until broccoli is tender. Serve chicken mixture over cooked rice.

Naomi Cooper, Delaware, OH

Crock O' Brats

Serve with hearty rye bread and homestyle applesauce sprinkled with cinnamon.

Makes 6 servings

20-oz. pkg. bratwurst
5 potatoes, peeled and cubed
1 tart apple, cored and cubed
1 onion, chopped
1/4 c. brown sugar, packed
27-oz. can sauerkraut, drained

Brown bratwurst in a large skillet over medium heat; reserve drippings. Slice bratwurst into one-inch pieces; set aside. Combine remaining ingredients in a slow cooker. Stir in bratwurst slices with pan drippings. Cover and cook on high setting for 4 to 6 hours, or until potatoes are tender.

★ BEER BRAISED ★ Bratwurst and knockwurst are German sausages often braised in dark German beer. Just place the sausages in a pan with enough beer to cover them halfway. Bring the beer to a simmer and cook until it has evaporated. Then continue browning the sausages in the pan, or cook them on a hot grill.

Caribbean Chicken & Veggies

Angela Murphy, Tempe AZ

Savory Spinach Soufflé

Try using Swiss cheese instead of Cheddar for something deliciously different.

Makes 12 servings

2 16-oz. pkgs. frozen chopped spinach, thawed and well drained
1/4 c. onion, grated
8-oz. pkg. 1/3-less-fat cream cheese, softened
1/2 c. reduced-fat mayonnaise
1/2 c. shredded reduced-fat Cheddar cheese
2 eggs, beaten
1/4 t. pepper
1/8 t. nutmeg

In a bowl, mix together spinach and onion; set aside. In a separate bowl, beat together remaining ingredients until well blended; fold into spinach mixture. Spoon into a lightly greased slow cooker. Cover and cook on high setting for 2 to 3 hours, until set.

Cherylann Smith, Efland, NC

Best-Ever Lasagna

This is a quick, easy recipe for homestyle lasagna...just add garlic bread and a tossed salad.

Serves 6 to 8

1 lb. ground beef, browned and drained
1 t. Italian seasoning
8 lasagna noodles, uncooked and broken into thirds
28-oz. jar spaghetti sauce
1/3 c. water
4-oz. can sliced mushrooms, drained
15-oz. container ricotta cheese
8-oz. pkg. shredded mozzarella cheese
Garnish: shredded Parmesan cheese

Combine ground beef and Italian seasoning. Arrange half of the lasagna noodles in a greased slow cooker. Spread half of the ground beef mixture over noodles. Top with half each of remaining ingredients except Parmesan cheese. Repeat layering process. Cover and cook on low setting for 5 hours. Garnish with Parmesan cheese.

Savory Spinach Soufflé

Eileen Bennett, Jenison, MI

Help-Yourself Hamburger Casserole

Dinner is in the crock! This busy-day recipe is packed with healthy beef and vegetables. Everyone can fix their own plates while Mom is on the road, shuttling kids back & forth to school activities.

Makes 4 servings

1-1/2 lbs. lean ground beef
2 potatoes, peeled and sliced
1 to 3 carrots, peeled and sliced
15-oz. can peas, well drained
1 to 3 onions, sliced
2 stalks celery, sliced
salt and pepper to taste
10-3/4 oz. can tomato soup
1-1/4 c. water

Brown beef in a skillet over medium heat; drain and set aside. Meanwhile, in a slow cooker, layer vegetables in order given; season each layer with salt and pepper. Add beef on top of celery. Whisk together soup and water in a bowl; pour into slow cooker. Cover and cook on low setting for 6 to 8 hours, or on high setting for 2 to 4 hours, stirring occasionally.

★ HANDY TIP ★ Do your favorite slow-cooker recipes finish cooking a few hours before you get home? If your slow cooker doesn't have a timer setting, then you may want to prepare the ingredients the night before. If you refrigerate the filled crock overnight, it will take 2 to 3 hours longer to cook, which is perfect when you will be out & about all day!

Help-Yourself Hamburger Casserole

Ramona Storm, Gardner, IL

Easy Chicken & Noodles

This smells so good and warms you up on a cold day. Leftover cooked chicken works great. Add some warm, crusty bread and a citrus salad...dinner is served!

Makes 8 servings

16-oz. pkg. frozen egg noodles, uncooked
2 14-1/2 oz. cans chicken broth
2 10-3/4 oz. cans cream of chicken soup
1/2 c. onion, finely chopped
1/2 c. carrot, peeled and diced
1/2 c. celery, diced
salt and pepper to taste
2 c. boneless, skinless chicken breasts, cooked and cubed
cooked mashed potatoes, warmed

Thaw egg noodles (or run package under warm water) just enough to break apart; set aside. Spray a slow cooker with non-stick vegetable spray. Add remaining ingredients except chicken; blend well. Stir in noodles and chicken. Cover and cook on low setting for 7 to 8 hours, until hot and bubbly. Serve over warmed mashed potatoes.

Julie Klum, Lake Oswego, OR

Tammy's Italian Chicken

Everyone loves this quick & easy dish! My son gets a thumbs-up from the other firefighters on his crew when it's his turn to cook, and my sister-in-law got rave reviews when she served it to her son's high school football team.

Serves 4 to 6

2-1/2 lbs. frozen chicken breasts
1-1/2 oz. pkg. spaghetti sauce mix
14-1/2 oz. can diced tomatoes
8-oz. can tomato sauce
cooked penne pasta
Garnish: grated Parmesan cheese

Arrange frozen chicken in a slow cooker. Sprinkle with sauce mix; add tomatoes and tomato sauce. Cover and cook on low setting for 7 to 8 hours, or on high setting for 3-1/2 to 4-1/2 hours. Serve over penne pasta, sprinkled with Parmesan cheese.

★ DRESS IT UP ★ **Dress up instant mashed potatoes to serve alongside Easy Chicken & Noodles. Prepare a family-size portion, then stir in an 8-ounce package of cream cheese. Spoon into a baking dish and bake at 375 to 400 degrees for about 30 minutes, until golden.**

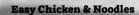
Easy Chicken & Noodles

Amy Butcher, Columbus, GA

Black-Eyed Peas & Ham Hock

Down-home goodness! We like it spicy, but if you don't, there are lots of other tasty flavors of diced tomatoes to choose from.

Serves 10 to 12

6 c. water
1 lb. dried black-eyed peas, rinsed and sorted
14-1/2 oz. can diced tomatoes with green chiles
14-1/2 oz. can diced tomatoes with jalapeño peppers
2 10-1/2 oz. cans chicken broth
1 stalk celery, chopped
salt and pepper to taste
1 ham hock

In a large saucepan over high heat, bring water to a boil. Add peas and return to a full boil; boil for 2 minutes. Remove from heat; let stand for one hour. Drain, discarding water. Add peas to a slow cooker. Stir in tomatoes with juice and remaining ingredients, pushing ham hock down into ingredients. Cover and cook on low setting for 8 to 10 hours, until peas are tender.

Dixie Dill, Elkland, MO

Mom's Classic Cabbage Rolls

My mom gave me this recipe when I was a frazzled newlywed. It's simple and delicious, especially good on a cold winter day.

Serves 4 to 6

1-1/2 lbs. ground beef
1/2 c. instant rice, uncooked
1 egg
1 t. garlic powder
1/2 t. salt
1/2 t. pepper
1 onion, diced
12 to 14 cabbage leaves

In a bowl, mix together uncooked beef and remaining ingredients except cabbage leaves; set aside. Drop cabbage leaves into boiling water for 3 to 4 minutes, until pliable; drain. Place 1/4 cup beef mixture in the center of each leaf. Fold in sides and roll up; set aside. Pour half the Tomato Sauce into a slow cooker; add cabbage rolls. Pour remaining sauce over rolls. Cover and cook on high setting for 5 to 6 hours.

Tomato Sauce:

2 8-oz. cans tomato sauce
juice of 2 lemons
3 T. all-purpose flour
1/2 c. sugar

Combine all ingredients in a bowl; mix well.

Black-Eyed Peas & Ham Hock

Diane Tracy, Lake Mary, FL

Chicken Parmigiana

This is incredibly delicious...so tender you won't need a knife!

Makes 6 servings

1 egg
3/4 c. 1% low-fat milk
1/2 t. salt
1/2 t. pepper
3/4 c. Italian-seasoned dry bread
   crumbs
3 6-oz. boneless, skinless chicken
   breasts, cut in half
1 T. olive oil
26-oz. jar spaghetti sauce, divided
3/4 c. shredded part-skim mozzarella
   cheese
3 c. cooked spaghetti

Beat together egg and milk in a deep bowl. Add salt and pepper; set aside. Place bread crumbs in a shallow bowl. Dip chicken breasts into egg mixture; coat with crumb mixture. Spray both sides of chicken with non-stick vegetable cooking spray. Heat oil in a skillet over medium heat; cook chicken just until golden on both sides. Add one cup sauce to the bottom of a slow cooker; top with chicken. Spoon remaining sauce over chicken. Cover and cook on low setting for 6 to 8 hours. About 15 minutes before serving, sprinkle cheese over top; cover until melted. Serve chicken and sauce over cooked spaghetti.

★ SKINNY SECRET ★ For a delicious, healthy change from pasta, make "noodles" from zucchini and summer squash! Cut squash into long, thin strips or strings, then steam lightly or sauté in a little olive oil. Add your favorite spaghetti sauce...yummy!

Chicken Parmigiana

Angela Murphy, Tempe AZ

Dijon-Ginger Carrots

Tangy mustard and ginger, sweet brown sugar...I just adore this super-simple dressed-up carrot recipe! Garnish with snipped fresh chives or mint.

Makes 12 servings

12 carrots, peeled and sliced 1/4-inch
    thick
1/3 c. Dijon mustard
1/2 c. brown sugar, packed
1 t. fresh ginger, peeled and minced
1/4 t. salt
1/8 t. pepper

Combine all ingredients in a slow cooker; stir. Cover and cook on high setting for 2 to 3 hours, until carrots are tender, stirring twice during cooking.

Susan Butters, Bountiful, UT

Pintos & Pork Over Corn Chips

A hearty dish that feeds a crowd of hungry people...easily!

Makes 10 servings

16-oz. pkg. dried pinto beans, rinsed
    and sorted
3-lb. pork loin roast, trimmed
7 c. water
4-oz. can chopped green chiles
1/2 c. onion, chopped
2 cloves garlic, minced
2 T. chili powder
1 T. ground cumin
1 T. salt
1 t. dried oregano
Garnish: corn chips, sour cream,
    shredded Cheddar cheese, chopped
    tomatoes, shredded lettuce

Cover beans with water in a large soup pot; soak overnight. Drain. Add beans and remaining ingredients except garnish to a slow cooker. Cover and cook on low setting for 9 hours. Remove roast, discarding bones; return to slow cooker. Cook, uncovered, for 30 minutes, until thickened. Serve over corn chips; garnish as desired.

Dijon-Ginger Carrots

Jessica Shrout, Flintstone, MD

Slow-Cooker Scalloped Potatoes

A rich and cheesy adaptation of a favorite baked recipe. It's wonderful for potlucks and get-togethers. Sometimes I'll add a few unpeeled, sliced redskin potatoes for a bit of color.

Makes 8 to 10 servings

4 lbs. potatoes, peeled, sliced and divided
2 T. butter, sliced
1 onion, diced and divided
16-oz. pkg. thick-cut bacon, diced and divided
3 c. shredded Cheddar cheese, divided
8-oz. pkg. cream cheese, cubed and divided
2 10-3/4 oz. cans cream of chicken soup
dried parsley, salt and pepper to taste

Arrange half of the potato slices in a large slow cooker; dot with butter. Top with half each of the onion, uncooked bacon and cheeses; repeat layers. Top with soup and seasonings. Cover and cook on low setting for 8 to 10 hours, until bubbly and potatoes are tender.

Mary Alice Veal, Mars Hill, NC

Slow-Cooked Mac & Cheese

This tastes just like the old-fashioned macaroni & cheese that Grandma used to make. It is delicious and oh-so easy!

Makes 6 to 8 servings

8-oz. pkg. elbow macaroni, cooked
2 eggs, beaten
12-oz. can evaporated milk
1-1/2 c. milk
3 c. shredded sharp Cheddar cheese
1/2 c. margarine, melted
1 t. salt
pepper to taste

Mix all ingredients together and pour into a lightly greased slow cooker. Cover and cook on low setting for 3 to 4 hours.

★ QUICK CLEAN-UP ★ For easy clean-up, spray the inside of your slow cooker with non-stick vegetable spray before adding ingredients. You'll be glad you did!

Slow-Cooker Scalloped Potatoes

Vickie, Gooseberry Patch

Southwestern Pork Chalupas

You're going to love this zesty dish! I like to serve it with a chopped tomato and avocado salad.

Makes 10 servings

2 15-oz. cans pinto beans, drained and rinsed
4-oz. can chopped green chiles
4 c. water
2 T. chili powder
2 t. ground cumin
1 t. dried oregano
1 t. salt
1 t. pepper to taste
2-lb. pork shoulder roast
9-oz. pkg. multi-grain tortilla chips

Garnish: shredded Mexican-blend cheese, sour cream, salsa, sliced black olives, sliced jalapeño peppers

Combine beans, chiles, water and spices in a large slow cooker; mix well. Add roast; cover and cook on low setting for 4 hours. Remove roast and shred, discarding any bones; return pork to slow cooker. Cover and cook on low setting for an additional 2 to 4 hours, adding more water if necessary. To serve, arrange tortilla chips on serving plates. Spoon pork mixture over chips; garnish as desired.

★ SLOW-COOKED ★ Want to use dried beans instead of canned in a recipe? They are easy to prepare in your slow cooker. Instead of soaking, dried beans can be slow-cooked overnight on low. Cover with water and add a teaspoon of baking soda. In the morning, simply drain and they're ready to use.

Southwestern Pork Chalupas

Lisa Hays, Crocker, MO

Garden-Style Fettuccine

What a delicious, nutritious meatless meal! It's packed full of veggies and yummy cheese...what more could you ask for?

Makes 12 servings

1 zucchini, sliced 1/4-inch thick
1 yellow squash, sliced 1/4-inch thick
2 carrots, peeled and thinly sliced
1-1/2 c. sliced mushrooms
10-oz. pkg. frozen broccoli cuts
4 green onions, sliced
1 clove garlic, minced
1/2 t. dried basil
1/4 t. salt
1/2 t. pepper
1 c. grated Parmesan cheese
12-oz. pkg. fettuccine pasta, cooked
1 c. shredded mozzarella cheese
1 c. 1% low-fat milk
2 egg yolks, beaten

Place vegetables, seasonings and Parmesan cheese in a slow cooker. Cover and cook on high setting for 2 hours. Add remaining ingredients to slow cooker; stir well. Reduce heat to low setting; cover and cook an additional 15 to 30 minutes.

Julie Neff, Citrus Springs, FL

Herb Garden Chicken

This is the chicken dish my husband asks for most often. I'm happy to oblige because it's so tasty and so easy to put together.

Serves 4 to 6

4 to 6 boneless, skinless chicken breasts
2 tomatoes, chopped
1 onion, chopped
2 cloves garlic, chopped
2/3 c. chicken broth
1 bay leaf
1 t. dried thyme
1-1/2 t. salt
1 t. pepper, or more to taste
2 c. broccoli flowerets
Optional: 2 to 3 T. all-purpose flour
cooked rice

Place chicken in a slow cooker; top with tomatoes, onion and garlic. In a bowl, combine broth and seasonings; pour over chicken mixture. Cover and cook on low setting for 8 hours. Add broccoli; cook for one additional hour, or until chicken juices run clear and broccoli is tender. Juices in slow cooker may be thickened with flour, if desired. Discard bay leaf; serve chicken and vegetables over cooked rice.

Garden-Style Fettuccine

Tami Hoffman, Litchfield, NH

Slow-Cooker Creamy Apricot Chicken

Serve with creamy mashed potatoes and your favorite veggie. Then pour on spoonfuls of the creamy apricot sauce.

Serves 4 to 6

1 to 2 lbs. boneless, skinless chicken breasts
12-oz. jar apricot preserves
8-oz. bottle Russian salad dressing

Arrange chicken in a 4-quart slow cooker; set aside. Combine preserves and salad dressing; spoon over chicken. Cover and cook on high setting for one hour. Reduce heat to low and cook for 3 hours, or until chicken juices run clear.

Jean Carter, Rockledge, FL

Swiss Steak

I have served this for years to a variety of very picky eaters...they all loved it! Serve with buttery mashed potatoes.

Serves 4 to 6

2-lb. boneless beef round steak, cut into 4 to 6 serving-size pieces
1.1-oz. pkg. beefy onion soup mix
3 c. onion, sliced
28-oz. can diced tomatoes
3 T. all-purpose flour
1 c. water
Garnish: minced fresh parsley

Arrange steak in a slow cooker. Sprinkle soup mix over steak; arrange onion slices all around. Top with undrained tomatoes. Cover and cook on low setting for 8 hours, or on high setting for 4 hours. Remove steak and vegetables to a serving dish; set aside. Mix together flour and water in a small bowl; add to juices in slow cooker and stir until thickened. Spoon gravy over steak to serve. Sprinkle with parsley.

Slow Cooker Creamy Apricot Chicken

Debi Finnen, Berlin Heights, OH

Slow-Cooker Pepper Steak

This is a good recipe to make when onions and peppers are plentiful in your backyard garden.

Makes 8 servings

2 lbs. beef sirloin, cut into bite-size
    strips
garlic powder to taste
3 T. oil
1 cube beef bouillon
1/4 c. boiling water
1 T. cornstarch
1/2 c. onion, chopped
2 green peppers, thinly sliced
14-oz. can stewed tomatoes

3 T. reduced-sodium soy sauce
1 t. sugar
1 t. salt
4 c. cooked brown rice

Sprinkle beef with garlic powder. In a large skillet over medium heat, brown beef in oil. Transfer to a slow cooker. Mix together bouillon cube and water until dissolved; stir in cornstarch until dissolved. Pour over beef. Stir in remaining ingredients except rice. Cover and cook on low setting for 6 to 8 hours, or on high setting for 3 to 4 hours. Serve over rice.

★ BEST BET ★ Make sure to use the right-size slow cooker...they cook their best when at least half of the crock is filled.

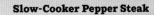

Slow-Cooker Pepper Steak

Louise Greer, Cartersville, GA

Spicy Peaches with Raspberry Sauce

Your house will smell so inviting with this simple yet incredibly good dish simmering away!

Makes 12 servings

2 29-oz. cans peach halves in syrup
cinnamon, nutmeg and ground
    cloves to taste
2 c. light brown sugar, packed
2 T. butter, diced
1 T. vanilla extract
Optional: raisins, prunes, figs or
    dates
Garnish: vanilla ice cream, warmed
    raspberry sauce, fresh raspberries

Combine undrained peaches and remaining ingredients except garnish in a slow cooker; stir gently to mix. Cover and cook on high setting for 2 hours, until peaches are glazed and tender. To serve, place a scoop of ice cream in each bowl; top with 2 peach halves and a generous serving of raspberry sauce and a few fresh raspberries.

Fawn McKenzie, Wenatchee, WA

Autumn Apple-Pecan Dressing

Made in the slow cooker, this side dish frees up your oven for a tasty roast chicken.

Makes 12 servings

4 c. soft bread cubes
1 c. saltine crackers, crushed
1-1/2 c. apples, peeled, cored and
    chopped
1 c. chopped pecans
1 c. onion, chopped
1 c. celery, chopped
2/3 c. low-sodium chicken broth
1/4 c. butter, melted
2 eggs, beaten
1/2 t. pepper
1/2 t. dried sage

Combine bread cubes, cracker crumbs, apples, pecans, onion and celery in a slow cooker; set aside.
In a small bowl, mix remaining ingredients until well blended. Pour into slow cooker and toss to coat. Cover and cook on low setting for 4 to 5 hours, until dressing is puffed and golden around edges.

Spicy Peaches with Raspberry Sauce

Carolyn Deckard, Bedford IN

Tamale Casserole

Another easy meal you can put together and let cook while you work or play. I always serve a lettuce salad with it.

Makes 6 servings

1 lb. lean ground beef
1 egg, beaten
1-1/2 c. 2% reduced-fat milk
3/4 c. cornmeal
14-1/2 oz. can diced tomatoes
15-1/4 oz. can corn, drained
2-1/2 oz. can sliced black olives, drained
1-oz. pkg. chili seasoning mix
1/2 t. seasoned salt
1 c. shredded reduced-fat Cheddar cheese

In a skillet over medium heat, cook beef until no longer pink; drain. Meanwhile, in a bowl, combine egg, milk and cornmeal. Stir until smooth; add tomatoes with juice, corn, olives, seasoning mix and seasoned salt. Add beef; stir well and spoon into a slow cooker sprayed with non-stick vegetable spray. Cover and cook on high setting for 3 hours and 45 minutes. Sprinkle with cheese. Cover and cook 15 minutes longer, or until cheese is melted.

★ MAKE IT YOURS ★ Fill a muffin tin with fixings like diced tomatoes, chopped green onion, extra sliced olives and diced avocado...everyone can top their own Tamale Casserole to their liking.

Tamale Casserole

Sandra Sullivan, Aurora, CT

Chicken with Artichokes & Capers

Quick, easy and a hit with the whole family! Add a simple side salad and warm bread...you'll have a gourmet dinner in no time.

Serves 6 to 8

3 lbs. boneless, skinless chicken
  thighs
salt and pepper to taste
14-1/2 oz. can diced tomatoes
14-oz. can artichoke hearts, drained
1/4 c. capers
2 to 3 cloves garlic, thinly sliced
3 tomatoes, chopped
8-oz. pkg. sliced mushrooms
16-oz. pkg. spaghetti, cooked

Season chicken with salt and pepper; place in a slow cooker. Spoon canned tomatoes with juice, artichokes, capers and garlic over chicken. Cover and cook on high setting for 3 to 4 hours, until chicken juices run clear. Stir in fresh tomatoes and mushrooms during the last 30 minutes of cooking. Serve chicken and sauce over spaghetti.

Leslie McKinley, Macomb, MO

Mike's Irresistible Italian Chops

My dad is a master at cooking meats, and this is one of his signature dishes! We enjoy these chops with buttered noodles, rice or couscous.

Makes 5 servings

5 pork chops
1-1/2 onions, coarsely chopped
15-oz. can stewed tomatoes
1/3 c. oil
1-1/2 t. Italian seasoning
1-1/2 t. garlic powder
2 t. smoke-flavored cooking sauce
1/4 c. water

Layer chops and onions in a slow cooker; add tomatoes with juice and remaining ingredients. Cover and cook on low setting for 3 to 4 hours, until chops are tender.

★ SPICE IT UP ★ To add extra flavor, sprinkle pork chops or beef with a little bit of this simple seasoning before adding to your slow cooker: combine one cup salt, 1/4 cup pepper and 1/4 cup garlic powder. Mix all together and store in an airtight container for up to 6 months.

Chicken with Artichokes & Capers

JoAnn's Chocolate Bread Pudding, Page 230

CHAPTER SIX

Warm & Cozy Desserts

Honeyed Apple Treat, Page 244

Lemon-Poppy Seed Cake, Page 232

Audra Vanhorn-Sorey, Columbia, NC

S'mores Cobbler

A unique twist on a family favorite... it's sure to be a hit!

Makes 10 servings

5-oz. pkg. cook & serve chocolate
   pudding mix
1 c. whole milk
6 whole graham crackers, broken
   in half
1/2 c. mini semi-sweet chocolate
   chips
18-1/2 oz. pkg. chocolate cake mix
1/2 c. butter, sliced
10-oz. pkg. marshmallows

Prepare pudding mix with milk according to package directions; cool slightly. Spoon pudding into an ungreased 13"x9" baking pan. Arrange graham crackers over pudding, with some space between crackers. Sprinkle with chocolate chips; spread dry cake mix over top and dot with butter. Bake at 350 degrees for 25 minutes. Remove from oven; stir slightly to ensure all ingredients are moistened. Top with marshmallows. Bake for an additional 8 to 10 minutes, until marshmallows are melted.

Karen Norman, Jacksonville, FL

Sweet Mini Apple Dumplings

Delicious served with a scoop of vanilla ice cream!

Makes 32 dumplings

2 8-oz. tubes refrigerated crescent
   rolls, separated
4 apples, peeled, cored and sliced into
   8 wedges
1/2 c. butter
1 c. sugar
1 c. water
1/2 t. cinnamon

Cut each crescent roll in half, forming 2 triangles from each; roll up one apple wedge in each triangle crescent-roll style. Arrange in a 13"x9" baking pan coated with non-stick vegetable spray; set aside. Add butter, sugar and water to a small saucepan; bring to a boil. Reduce heat; boil and stir until sugar dissolves. Pour over crescents; bake at 350 degrees for 30 minutes. Sprinkle with cinnamon.

S'mores Cobbler

Marilyn Just, De Soto, KS

Aunt Marge's Peachy Pineapple Dessert

This recipe is at least 50 years old. It was handed down to my mom from a very close family friend we called Aunt Marge. It was my favorite dessert growing up.

Serves 10 to 12

20-oz. can crushed pineapple
29-oz. can sliced peaches
18-1/2 oz. pkg. white or yellow
   cake mix
1/2 to 1 c. chopped walnuts or pecans
3/4 to 1 c. butter, melted

In an ungreased 13"x9" glass baking pan, evenly spread pineapple with juices; add peaches with juices. Sprinkle with dry cake mix, then with nuts. Drizzle with melted butter; do not stir. Bake at 350 degrees for 35 to 40 minutes, until bubbly and top is lightly golden. Serve warm.

Gerry Donnella, Boston, VA

Tried & True Apple Casserole

My family loves these easy baked apples.

Makes 8 servings

8 to 10 tart apples, peeled, cored and
   halved
1/2 c. sugar
1 T. all-purpose flour
1/2 t. cinnamon
1/4 t. nutmeg
1 T. butter, diced
Optional: golden raisins, chopped
   walnuts

Place apples in a greased 2-quart casserole dish; set aside. Mix together dry ingredients; sprinkle over apples. Dot with butter. Sprinkle with raisins and walnuts, if desired. Cover and bake at 350 degrees for 45 minutes to one hour.

★ SAVVY SECRET ★ For delicious apple desserts, some of the best apple varieties are Granny Smith, Gala and Jonathan as well as old-timers like Rome Beauty, Northern Spy and Winesap. But ask at the orchard...the grower is sure to have tips for you!

Aunt Marge's Peachy Pineapple Dessert

Gail Girard, Cumberland, RI

Old-Fashioned Indian Pudding

This is a rich, old-fashioned pudding we used to enjoy when I was a child. It's wonderful to serve on a crisp fall day. It brings back memories of raking leaves and playing with friends.

Makes 8 servings

6 c. 1% milk
1/2 c. butter, sliced
1/2 c. yellow cornmeal
1/4 c. all-purpose or whole-wheat
   flour
1 t. salt
1/2 c. molasses
3 eggs
1/3 c. sugar
1 t. cinnamon
1/2 t. ground ginger
1/2 t. nutmeg
Optional: 1 c. raisins, dried
   cranberries or chopped dried
   apples
Garnish: vanilla ice cream or
   whipped cream

In a large saucepan over medium-high heat, heat milk just to boiling. Watch carefully to avoid scorching. Reduce heat to medium; add butter. In a bowl, mix cornmeal, flour, salt and molasses. Stir 1/2 cup of hot milk into cornmeal mixture. Add cornmeal mixture to hot milk in pan. Cook and stir over medium heat until thickened. In a separate bowl, beat eggs; whisk in 1/2 cup of hot milk mixture. Pour egg mixture into the pan. Add sugar and spices; stir until smooth. Add fruit, if using. Pour mixture into a greased 2-1/2 quart casserole dish. Bake, uncovered, at 250 degrees for 2 hours. Cool for about one hour. Garnish as desired.

★ SWEET TIP ★ Light molasses has a sweet, mild taste best for biscuits, waffles and pancakes. But for baking, "dark" molasses, which is less sweet and thicker, is best. In a pinch, they can be interchanged, but to get that robust molasses flavor in a casserole, dark molasses is the best choice.

Old-Fashioned Indian Pudding

Wendell Mays, Barboursville, WV

Grandma's Peach Cobbler

This is an awesome recipe, one my grandmother made very often. We could eat it daily! The almond extract and sprinkle of cinnamon were Grandma's special touches. A great comfort food that's so simple, any honeymooner could make it.

Serves 6 to 8

1/2 c. butter, sliced
15-1/4 oz. can sliced peaches in
   syrup
1 c. self-rising flour
1 c. sugar
1 c. milk
1 t. almond extract
cinnamon to taste
Optional: whipping cream or
   vanilla ice cream

Add butter to an 11"x7" baking pan; melt in a 350-degree oven. Pour peaches with syrup into pan; set aside. In a bowl, combine flour, sugar, milk and extract; stir until smooth. Pour batter over peaches. Bake at 350 degrees until bubbly and golden, about 35 to 45 minutes. Remove from oven; immediately sprinkle with cinnamon. Serve warm, topped with cream or ice cream, if desired.

Christy Hughes, Provo, UT

Open-Face Peach Pie

This favorite pie recipe was handed down to me from my grandmother.

Makes 8 servings

1 c. sugar
2 T. cornstarch
9-inch pie crust
6 peaches, peeled, pitted and halved
1 c. whipping cream

Mix sugar and cornstarch together; spread 3/4 of mixture into pie crust. Arrange peaches on top; sprinkle with remaining sugar mixture. Pour cream evenly over peaches; bake at 400 degrees for 10 minutes. Reduce heat to 350 degrees; bake an additional 40 minutes.

★ EASY SWITCH ★ Out of peaches? Nectarines can be used in the same recipes as peaches. The only difference between the two is the lack of fuzz on the nectarine, and they tend to be a bit smaller in size.

Grandma's Peach Cobbler

Linda Belon, Wintersville, OH

Peanut Butter Apple Crisp

Scrumptious served warm, topped with generous scoops of smooth vanilla ice cream.

Serves 10 to 12

1 c. all-purpose flour
1-1/2 c. brown sugar, packed
1 t. cinnamon
3/4 c. creamy peanut butter
1/3 c. butter, softened
6 to 8 tart apples, peeled, cored and thinly sliced
2 T. lemon juice
1 t. lemon zest
Garnish: vanilla ice cream

Combine flour, brown sugar and cinnamon in a bowl. Cut in peanut butter and butter until mixture resembles coarse crumbs; set aside. Arrange apple slices in a lightly greased 13"x9" baking pan; sprinkle with lemon juice and zest. Top apples with crumb mixture. Bake at 350 degrees for 35 to 45 minutes. Serve warm, topped with a scoop of ice cream.

Elizabeth Wenk, Cuyahoga Falls, OH

Orange-Peach Dump Cake

A different flavor combination for this trusty dessert.

Serves 8 to 10

14-1/2 oz. can peach pie filling, chopped
18-oz. pkg. orange cake mix
2 eggs, beaten
1/2 c. sour cream

Combine all ingredients in an ungreased 13"x9" baking pan. Mix with a fork until well blended; smooth top. Bake at 350 degrees for 40 to 45 minutes.

★ BERRY GOOD ★ Blueberries, raspberries, mulberries and strawberries are all scrumptious. For a flavorful change, mix & match berries in dessert recipes for cakes, muffins, and quick bread recipes.

Peanut Butter Apple Crisp

Judy Lange, Imperial, PA

Almond Amaretto Bread Pudding

So simple to make, yet looks and tastes so special!

Makes 12 servings

1 qt. half-and-half
1 loaf Italian bread, cubed
3 eggs
1-1/2 c. sugar
2 T. almond extract
1 c. golden raisins
3/4 c. sliced almonds

In a large bowl, pour half-and-half over bread and stir gently. Cover and refrigerate 30 minutes to one hour. In a separate bowl, beat eggs until they begin to foam. Add sugar; mix well. Stir in almond extract, raisins and almonds. Add to bread mixture and mix well. Pour into a lightly greased 13"x9" baking pan. Bake at 325 degrees for 50 minutes. Serve warm with Amaretto Sauce.

Amaretto Sauce:

1/2 c. butter
1 c. powdered sugar
1 egg, beaten
1/4 c. amaretto liqueur, or 1 T. almond extract plus 3 T. water

Melt butter in a double boiler. Beat in remaining ingredients. Cook, stirring constantly, until mixture begins to thicken.

Sharon Demers, Delores, CO

Cherry-Pecan Bread Pudding

This old-fashioned bread pudding recipe is one of our favorites.

Makes 12 servings

2-lb. loaf French bread, cubed
6 c. 2% milk
1/2 c. plus 2 T. sugar, divided
6 eggs, beaten
2 t. vanilla extract
1/2 t. cinnamon
1/2 c. dried tart cherries
1/2 c. chopped pecans
1/4 c. butter, melted

Spread bread cubes on a baking sheet; let dry overnight. Combine milk and 5 tablespoons sugar in a saucepan over low heat. Heat to 120 degrees on a candy thermometer; remove from heat. Whisk together eggs, vanilla, cinnamon and remaining sugar in a large bowl. Stir in cherries and pecans. Slowly whisk half of milk mixture into egg mixture; add remaining milk mixture. Stir in bread cubes; toss to mix and let stand for 5 minutes. Mix in butter; transfer mixture to lightly greased 13"x9" baking pan. Bake at 350 degrees for 35 minutes, or until center is firm. Serve warm.

Almond Amaretto Bread Pudding

Jo Ann, Gooseberry Patch

JoAnn's Chocolate Bread Pudding

A luscious chocolate dessert that's easy to make. Your guests will love it and so will you!

Makes 8 servings

16-oz. loaf French or Italian bread, cubed
3 c. milk
1 c. whipping cream, divided
1/2 c. coffee-flavored liqueur
1 c. sugar
1 c. light brown sugar, packed
1/4 c. baking cocoa
6 eggs, lightly beaten
1 T. vanilla extract
2 t. almond extract
1-1/2 t. cinnamon
8-oz. pkg. semi-sweet baking chocolate, grated and divided

Spread bread cubes in a lightly greased 13"x9" baking pan; set aside. In a large bowl, whisk together milk, 1/4 cup cream and liqueur; set aside. In a separate bowl, combine sugars and cocoa; mix well. Add sugar mixture to milk mixture; stir well. In a small bowl, whisk together eggs, extracts and cinnamon; add to milk mixture and mix well. Reserve a little grated chocolate for garnish; stir in remaining chocolate. Pour mixture over cubed bread. Let stand, stirring occasionally, for about 20 minutes, until bread absorbs most of the milk mixture. Bake at 325 degrees for one hour, or until set and a knife tip inserted in the center tests clean. Whip remaining cream with an electric mixer on high speed until soft peaks form. Serve pudding warm or chilled, garnished with whipped cream and reserved chocolate.

★ TOP IT OFF ★ Nothing says farm-fresh flavor like dollops of whipped cream on a warm home-baked dessert. In a chilled bowl, with chilled beaters, beat a cup of whipping cream on high speed until soft peaks form. Stir in 2 teaspoons sugar and 2 teaspoons vanilla extract.

JoAnn's Chocolate Bread Pudding

Rogene Rogers, Bemidji, MN

Lemon-Poppy Seed Cake

Delicious served with a dollop of whipped cream.

Serves 10 to 12

15.8-oz. lemon-poppy seed bread mix
1 egg, beaten
8-oz. container sour cream
1-1/4 c. water, divided
1/2 c. sugar
1/4 c. lemon juice

Combine bread mix, egg, sour cream and 1/2 cup water in a bowl. Stir until well-moistened; spread in a lightly greased 3 to 4-quart slow cooker. Combine 3/4 cup water and remaining ingredients in a small saucepan; bring to a boil. Pour boiling mixture over batter in slow cooker. Cover and cook on high setting for 2 to 2-1/2 hours, until edges are golden. Turn off slow cooker; let cake cool in slow cooker for 30 minutes with lid ajar. When cool enough to handle, hold a large plate over top of slow cooker and invert to turn out cake.

Jan Alvey, Westerville, OH

Pineapple-Cherry Crisp

Quick & easy to make, and most of the ingredients can be kept in the pantry for a spur-of-the-moment treat. Can't beat that!

Serves 12 to 15

20-oz. can crushed pineapple, well
   drained
2 21-oz. cans cherry pie filling
18-1/2 oz. pkg. white cake mix
1/2 c. butter, thinly sliced
3/4 c. chopped pecans
Garnish: whipped cream or ice cream

Spread pineapple evenly in an ungreased 13"x9" baking pan. Spoon pie filling over pineapple. Sprinkle dry cake mix on top; dot with butter and top with pecans. Bake at 350 degrees for 45 minutes, or until bubbly and topping is golden. Serve warm or cooled, garnished as desired.

★ STOCK THE PANTRY ★ Stock up on cake mixes, pudding mixes and fruit pie fillings whenever they go on sale...mix & match to make all kinds of simply delicious desserts.

Lemon-Poppy Seed Cake

Shirley Kelly, Nashua, NH

Strawberry-Nectarine Cobbler

Make this refreshing cobbler with summer-ripe fruit...yum! Add a scoop of ice cream, if you like.

Makes 12 servings

6 to 8 nectarines, pitted and very
  thinly sliced
1/4 c. light brown sugar, packed
1 t. cinnamon
1/4 t. nutmeg
1 t. salt
2 c. fresh strawberries, hulled and
  halved
2 T. butter, sliced
1/2 c. sugar, divided
1 egg, beaten
1 T. baking powder
1 c. all-purpose flour
1 T. vanilla extract
1/2 c. milk

Combine nectarines, brown sugar, spices and salt in a bowl; let stand for 15 minutes. In a saucepan over low heat, combine strawberries, butter and 1/4 cup sugar. Cook and stir for 5 minutes, until syrupy. Remove from heat; cool. In another bowl, whisk together egg, remaining sugar, baking powder, flour, vanilla and milk. Spread nectarine mixture evenly in an ungreased 13"x9" glass baking pan. Spoon strawberry mixture evenly over nectarines. Dollop with spoonfuls of batter. Bake at 350 degrees for 30 to 35 minutes. Cool at least 15 minutes before serving.

★ SWEET TREAT ★ Create a caramel delight to drizzle over ice cream, fruit or cobbler. Heat sugar in a saucepan over medium heat until it begins to turn golden brown...spoon over desserts for a sweet treat.

Strawberry-Nectarine Cobbler

Jill Burton, Gooseberry Patch

Slow-Cooker Caramel Apple Delight

Serve this sweet, gooey delight over vanilla ice cream or slices of angel food cake.

Makes 4 to 6 servings

1/2 c. apple juice
7-oz. pkg. caramels, unwrapped
1 t. vanilla extract
1/2 t. cinnamon
1/3 c. creamy peanut butter
4 to 5 tart apples, peeled, cored
   and sliced

Combine apple juice, caramels, vanilla and cinnamon in a slow cooker. Add peanut butter; mix well. Add apples; cover and cook on low setting for 5 hours. Stir thoroughly, cover and cook on low setting one additional hour.

Sandy Bernards, Valencia, CA

Berry Crumble

Instant oatmeal is the key to the scrumptious topping.

Makes 6 servings

4 c. blackberries or blueberries
1 to 2 T. sugar
3 T. butter, softened
3 1-1/2 oz. pkgs. quick-cooking
   instant oats with maple and
   brown sugar

Toss berries and sugar together in an ungreased 9" pie plate; set aside. Cut butter into quick-cooking oats until coarse crumbs form; sprinkle over berries. Bake at 375 degrees about 30 to 35 minutes until topping is golden.

★ QUICK & COOL ★ For a quick, cool dessert, layer blackberries, vanilla yogurt and crushed graham crackers in a crystal bowl.

Slow-Cooker Caramel Apple Delight

Barbara Burke, Newport News, VA

The Easiest Rice Pudding

We love old-fashioned rice pudding, and this version made in the slow cooker is so simple! We like to sprinkle a little bit of cinnamon and sweetened flaked coconut over ours for extra flavor.

Makes 10 servings

8 c. whole milk
1 c. long-cooking brown rice, uncooked
1/2 c. sugar
3 eggs
1/4 c. light cream
3/4 c. dried cranberries
2 t. vanilla extract
1/2 t. cinnamon
1/4 t. salt

Spray a slow cooker with non-stick vegetable spray; set aside. In a bowl, combine milk, uncooked rice and sugar; mix well. Spoon milk mixture into slow cooker. Cover and cook on low setting for 5 hours, or until rice is tender. When rice is tender, beat together eggs, cream and remaining ingredients. Whisk 1/2 cup of milk mixture from slow cooker into egg mixture. Continue whisking in the milk mixture, 1/2 cup at a time, until only half remains in slow cooker. Spoon everything back into slow cooker; stir. Cover and cook on low setting for one hour.

★ ADD CRUNCH ★ Add a delicious crunch to rice pudding...just add 1/4 cup slivered, toasted almonds. You can also add a peeled and diced pear or apple during the last few minutes of cooking for a brand new twist on an old favorite.

The Easiest Rice Pudding

Donna Elliott, Winchester, TN

Cup of Cobbler

My simple fruit cobbler recipe tastes as good as my granny's!

Serves 4 to 6

1/2 c. butter, sliced
1 c. all-purpose flour
1 c. sugar
1 c. milk
15-oz. can sliced peaches, cherries
  or blackberries in syrup

Add butter to a lightly greased one-quart casserole dish; melt in a 350-degree oven. In a bowl, stir together flour, sugar and milk; pour batter into melted butter. Pour undrained fruit over top; do not stir. Bake at 350 degrees for 30 to 40 minutes, until bubbly and golden. Serve warm.

Arlene Smulski, Lyons, IL

Chocolate-Cherry Cobbler

Top with dollops of whipped cream...luscious!

Serves 4 to 6

1/4 c. butter, melted
1/2 t. vanilla extract
30-oz. can cherry pie filling
1 c. all-purpose flour
1 c. sugar
1-1/2 t. baking powder
1/4 c. baking cocoa
1/2 c. milk

In a small bowl, combine melted butter and vanilla; spread mixture in a 13"x9" baking pan. Pour pie filling into pan; set aside. In a bowl, mix together flour, sugar, baking powder and cocoa. Stir in milk. Pour batter over pie filling; do not stir. Bake at 350 degrees for 30 to 40 minutes, until golden. Serve warm.

★ QUICK TIP ★ Canned fruit pie filling is different from canned fruit in syrup...be sure to double-check which kind is called for in cobbler & crisp recipes.

Cup of Cobbler

Donna Borton, Columbus, OH

Pumpkin Custard Crunch

I have made this festive dessert for years. Enjoy it plain or topped with ice cream like my husband does!

Serves 9 to 12

29-oz. can pumpkin
3 eggs, beaten
2 t. pumpkin pie spice
1 t. cinnamon
14-oz. can sweetened condensed
　milk
1 c. milk
2 t. vanilla extract

Mix pumpkin, eggs and spices well; stir in milks and vanilla. Pour into a greased 13"x9" baking pan; spoon Crunch Topping over pumpkin mixture. Bake at 350 degrees for 45 to 60 minutes, until a knife tip comes out clean. Watch carefully so that topping doesn't burn. Serve warm.

Crunch Topping:

3 c. quick-cooking oats, uncooked
1 c. brown sugar, packed
1 c. all-purpose flour
1 t. cinnamon
1 c. walnuts or pecans, crushed
1 c. butter, melted

Stir together oats, brown sugar, flour, cinnamon and nuts. Add melted butter; toss to mix.

Beth Ratcliff, West Des Moines, IA

Peaches & Cream Dessert

Peaches never tasted so good!

Makes 9 servings

3/4 c. all-purpose flour
3-1/2 oz. pkg. instant vanilla pudding
　mix
1 t. baking powder
1 egg, beaten
1/2 c. milk
3 T. butter, melted and slightly cooled
16-oz. can sliced peaches, drained
　and 1/3 c. juice reserved
8-oz. pkg. cream cheese, softened
1/2 c. plus 1 T. sugar, divided
1/2 t. cinnamon

In a bowl, combine flour, dry pudding mix and baking powder; set aside. In a separate bowl, blend egg, milk and butter together; add to flour mixture. Mix well; spread in a greased 8"x8" baking pan. Chop peaches and sprinkle over batter; set aside. Blend cream cheese, 1/2 cup sugar and reserved peach juice together until smooth; pour over peaches. Mix remaining sugar and cinnamon together; sprinkle on top. Bake at 350 degrees for 45 minutes.

Pumpkin Custard Crunch

Connie Bryant, Topeka, KS

Honeyed Apple Treat

This dessert is one my friend Ellen shared with our family when I was feeling a bit under the weather. She brought along a dozen fresh eggs from her hens as well...what a farmgirl!

Makes 8 servings

4 tart apples, peeled, cored and sliced
2 c. low-fat granola with raisins
1/4 c. honey
2 T. butter, melted
1 t. cinnamon
1/2 t. nutmeg
Optional: whipped topping,
   additional nutmeg

Combine apples and granola in a slow cooker. In a separate bowl, combine honey, butter, cinnamon and nutmeg; pour over apple mixture and mix well. Cover and cook on low setting for 8 hours. Garnish servings with a dollop of whipped topping and sprinkle with additional nutmeg, if desired.

Brenda Smith, Delaware, OH

Brenda's Fruit Crisp

Here's my favorite dessert recipe...it's a yummy way to use a bumper crop of peaches, apples or berries!

Makes 6 servings

5 c. frozen peaches, apples or berries,
   thawed and juices reserved
1 T. sugar
1/2 c. long-cooking oats, uncooked
1/3 c. brown sugar, packed
1/4 c. all-purpose flour
1/4 t. vanilla extract
1/4 t. nutmeg
1/4 t. cinnamon
1/4 c. unsweetened flaked coconut
1/3 c. butter, diced
Garnish: vanilla ice cream

Place fruit and reserved juices in an ungreased 2-quart casserole dish; stir in sugar and set aside. Mix oats, brown sugar, flour, vanilla and spices in a bowl. Stir in coconut. Add butter to oat mixture; mix with a fork until mixture is the texture of coarse crumbs. Sprinkle over fruit. Bake at 375 degrees for 30 to 35 minutes, until topping is golden and fruit is tender. Serve warm, topped with a scoop of ice cream.

Honeyed Apple Treat

Brenda Derby, Northborough, MA

Apple-Cranberry Crisp

We like to make this using several different varieties of tart baking apples.

Serves 10 to 12

6 c. apples, peeled, cored and
   sliced
3 c. cranberries
1 c. sugar
2 t. cinnamon
1 to 2 t. lemon juice
3/4 c. butter, sliced and divided
1 c. all-purpose flour
1 c. brown sugar, packed
Garnish: vanilla ice cream

Toss together apple slices, cranberries, sugar and cinnamon. Spread in a buttered 13"x9" glass baking pan. Sprinkle with lemon juice and dot with 1/4 cup butter. Blend remaining butter with flour and brown sugar until crumbly; sprinkle over apple mixture. Bake for one hour at 350 degrees. Serve warm with vanilla ice cream.

Apple-Cranberry Crisp

Mitzy LaFrenais-Hafner,
Quebec, Canada

Quebec Maple Bread Pudding

This bread pudding is cozy, quick & easy comfort food...wonderful when you are snowed in!

Makes 4 servings

3 c. egg bread or white bread,
  cubed
Optional: 1/2 c. chopped pecans
  or walnuts
3 c. milk
1 c. brown sugar, packed
4 eggs, beaten
1 t. vanilla extract
2 T. butter, sliced
Garnish: pure maple syrup

Place bread cubes in a greased 9"x9" baking pan. Sprinkle with nuts, if using; set aside. Combine milk and brown sugar in a saucepan over medium-low heat; stir until hot and sugar is dissolved. Remove from heat. Whisk in eggs; stir in vanilla. Pour milk mixture over bread, soaking thoroughly. Dot with butter. Bake at 350 degrees for one hour, or until set. Serve warm, drizzled generously with maple syrup.

Janis Parr, Ontario, Canada

Candy-Apple Tapioca

This yummy dessert is really two delectable desserts in one...creamy tapioca pudding and sweet cinnamon-spiced apples!

Makes 8 servings

8 McIntosh apples, peeled, cored
  and thinly sliced
2/3 c. sugar
1/4 c. instant tapioca, uncooked
3 T. red cinnamon candies
1/2 c. milk
Garnish: whipped cream

Place apples in a lightly greased slow cooker. In a bowl, stir together sugar, tapioca, candies and milk. Pour sugar mixture over apples. Cover and cook on high setting for 3 to 4 hours. Stir well before serving. Top servings with a dollop of whipped cream.

Quebec Maple Bread Pudding

Patricia Wissler, Harrisburg, PA

Country-Style Bread Pudding

This is the best-tasting bread pudding ever, and it's so much easier than making it in the oven.

Serves 8 to 10

3/4 c. brown sugar, packed
8 slices cinnamon-raisin bread,
   buttered and cubed
4 eggs, beaten
3-1/2 c. milk
1-1/2 t. vanilla extract
Garnish: whipped topping

Sprinkle brown sugar in a slow cooker that has been sprayed with non-stick vegetable spray. Add bread to slow cooker. Whisk together remaining ingredients except whipped cream; pour over bread. Cover and cook on high setting for 2 to 3 hours, until thickened. Do not stir. Spoon pudding into individual bowls. Drizzle brown sugar sauce from slow cooker over pudding. Garnish with dollops of whipped topping.

★ NUTTY TOPPING ★ Make a nutty dessert topping to spoon over bread pudding, ice cream or sliced pound cake. Mix a cup of toasted walnuts with a cup of maple syrup and place in a jar. Pecans and honey are scrumptious too. The topping may be stored at room temperature up to two weeks.

Country-Style Bread Pudding

Index

Sides

U. S. to Metric Recipe Equivalents

Volume Measurements

¼ teaspoon . . . . 1 mL
½ teaspoon . . . . 2 mL
1 teaspoon . . . . 5 mL
1 tablespoon = 3 teaspoons . . . . 15 mL
2 tablespoons = 1 fluid ounce . . . . 30 mL
¼ cup . . . . 60 mL
⅓ cup . . . . 75 mL
½ cup = 4 fluid ounces . . . . 125 mL
1 cup = 8 fluid ounces . . . . 250 mL
2 cups = 1 pint = 16 fluid ounces . . 500 mL
4 cups = 1 quart . . . . 1 L

Weights

1 ounce . . . . 30 g
4 ounces . . . . 120 g
8 ounces . . . . 225 g
16 ounces = 1 pound . . . . 450 g

Baking Pan Sizes

Square
8x8x2 inches . . . . 2 L = 20x20x5 cm
9x9x2 inches . . . . 2.5 L = 23x23x5 cm

Rectangular
13x9x2 inches . . . . 3.5 L = 33x23x5 cm

Loaf
9x5x3 inches . . . . 2 L = 23x13x7 cm

Round
8x1-1/2 inches . . . . 1.2 L = 20x4 cm
9x1-1/2 inches . . . . 1.5 L = 23x4 cm

Recipe Abbreviations

t. = teaspoon   ltr. = liter
T. = tablespoon   oz. = ounce
c. = cup   lb. = pound
pt. = pint   doz. = dozen
qt. = quart   pkg. = package
gal. = gallon   env. = envelope

Oven Temperatures

300˚ F . . . . 150° C
325˚ F . . . . 160° C
350˚ F . . . . 180° C
375˚ F . . . . 190° C
400˚ F . . . . 200° C
450˚ F . . . . 230° C

Kitchen Measurements

A pinch = ⅛ tablespoon
1 fluid ounce = 2 tablespoons
3 teaspoons = 1 tablespoon
4 fluid ounces = ½ cup
2 tablespoons = ⅛ cup
8 fluid ounces = 1 cup
4 tablespoons = ¼ cup
16 fluid ounces = 1 pint
8 tablespoons = ½ cup
32 fluid ounces = 1 quart
16 tablespoons = 1 cup
16 ounces net weight = 1 pound
2 cups = 1 pint
4 cups = 1 quart
4 quarts = 1 gallon